Leadership and control

A governance manual
for board members

Written by
Peter Davey, Radojka Miljevic
and James Tickell

NATIONAL
HOUSING
FEDERATION

Acknowledgements

This manual was originally known as the *Committee Members' Handbook*. It was rewritten as *In control* in 1996 by Julian Ashby, and subsequently revised by him in 2000 and 2004. This completely revised edition is by Peter Davey, Radojka Miljevic and James Tickell of Campbell Tickell.

ISBN 978 0 86297 566 1

First published as *In control* in 1996, revised first in September 2000, second in March 2005 by the National Housing Federation
2nd edition March 2011
Lion Court, 25 Procter Street London WC1V 6NY

Production Editor Fiona Shand

Printed in Great Britain by Typecast Colour, Hop Pocket Lane, Paddock Wood, Kent TN12 6DQ

Contents

Foreword

Good governance has been on the National Housing Federation's agenda for decades. This book appears at a time of continuing change and instability for Federation members, which will place growing demands on the quality of their governance. A new framework for regulation and funding was created, and has now swiftly been set aside by a government committed to further change. Public funding is being cut to the bone as the national deficit is tackled, with local authorities facing the need to make dramatic reductions in some services. Impoverished tenants and communities will be at the sharp end.

Associations face wider competition, and difficult decisions about rents, development, and how best to support deprived people and communities. Under the new framework, those organisations wishing to develop new homes need to consider increasing their rents, in some cases up to 80 per cent of market level. Meanwhile, the 'rules of the game' continue to change, sometimes in unpredictable ways. The Government's Big Society agenda plays to the strengths of associations, but may create new expectations of them.

This all adds up to unprecedented pressures on the quality of decision-making expected from the boards and board members of Federation members. The old 'passive' style of governance is no longer what is needed. Boards need to take a proactive approach, setting the agenda, challenging and supporting their officers, and managing the risks that are inherent in the emerging new framework.

The skills and experience of board members need to be honed for the challenges ahead. There can no longer be room for non-contributors and poor attendees on boards, whether they be nominated, elected or selected. Appraisal mechanisms need to be focused and hard-edged. The leadership role of each board needs greater emphasis, to ensure that the social mission and values are preserved, even at a time when greater commerciality is most needed.

All this adds up to a challenging, but perhaps exciting, time for the boards of Federation members. The demand for social housing is certain to rise, just as it becomes harder and riskier to provide new homes. There is scope for innovation, new partnerships, and new ways of working with tenants and in neighbourhoods. Local authorities may have reduced funds, but their influence and strategic role is on the increase.

For board members, information is power, to be exercised for the common good. This book aims to give them the information they need to get going on their vital jobs.

Chapter A

Introduction

Over the last 20 years the National Housing Federation has supported its member organisations in the ever-more demanding area of governance. There are now a number of publications available from the Federation, as well as training courses, model rules and the revised and very well received *Excellence in governance: Code for members and good practice guidance,* revised edition, 2010. The Federation also runs the Get on Board scheme which aims to match potential board members to vacancies on the boards of member organisations.

This completely new edition of the best-selling board members' handbook has been fully revised to reflect current legislation and good practice in the sector. It also reflects the new political and social context in which we all work and which you as board members operate. We hope that you will find this book a valuable tool in getting the most out of what is a challenging and rewarding role. This first chapter is for background reading and setting the overall context.

A1 Terminology

This book is aimed at the board members of all Federation members, whether they are housing associations or other kinds of social landlord. Housing associations are referred to in the text as a shorthand for the more unwieldy and technically correct 'social landlords which are not profit-distributing'.

The authors have tried, wherever possible, to avoid using housing jargon but, unavoidably, there are some particular organisations and phrases that need some explanation. See also the comprehensive jargon guide produced by the National Housing Federation (*Housing jargon: 7th edition*). Below are descriptions of the key players and phrases that board members need to be familiar with.

Affordable housing	An old phrase, but sometimes used now with a new meaning. Until recently, 'affordable housing' meant pretty much the same as 'social housing'. It may now refer to housing let on rents set at up to 80 per cent of market level, so as to generate funds for new development.
Audit Commission	The government body responsible (among other things) for the inspection of all social landlords against a set of standards known as Key Lines of Enquiry (KLOEs). The Commission is to be abolished from April 2012, when new arrangements will come into force. The full details of the new arrangements are yet to be published, but they will give a greater role to tenants and local elected representatives.
Charity Commission	The statutory body registering most charities, but not exempt charities (such as industrial and provident societies – see below). It has a responsibility for regulating the activities of organisations with charitable objectives.
Communities and Local Government (CLG)	The government department responsible for local government and housing.
Co-regulation	The approach to regulation of housing taken by the Tenant Services Authority (TSA) – see below. Co-regulation is a hands-off approach, which sets certain standards, but leaves the landlord to work out with its tenants and other stakeholders how best to achieve them. This approach is likely to continue beyond the abolition of the TSA.

Decent Homes	A minimum standard of housing repair (including modern bathrooms and kitchens), which the previous government had originally required housing associations and local authorities to meet by 2010. Some organisations have still to meet the standard on all of their housing stock.
Financial Services Authority (FSA)	The regulatory authority for all organisations providing financial services, including banks and brokers. When set up, it integrated the work of various statutory and other regulators. The Registry of Friendly Societies is now a part of the FSA, and regulates industrial and provident societies (see below).
Homes and Communities Agency (HCA)	The government's agency for the funding of social housing development and regeneration. From April 2012, the HCA will also assume the TSA's regulatory responsibilities.
Housing Corporation	The former government agency which funded and regulated housing associations. Abolished from December 2008, when the TSA and the HCA were created.
Industrial and Provident Society (I&P)	A mutual form of incorporation used by many housing associations, which may be charitable or non charitable. I&P societies are registered with the Financial Services Authority (see above).
Local offer	Social landlords are expected by the TSA to work with their tenants on a 'local offer' of services and support, which goes beyond the National Standards.
National Housing Federation	The national representative body for housing associations and other not-for-profit social landlords in England, and the publisher of this book.
National Standards	The performance standards created by the TSA for all social landlords. Likely to remain in force after the TSA is abolished.
Registered provider	An organisation (which can be public sector, private sector or not-for-profit) registered with the Tenant Services Authority.
Social housing	Another old phrase with a specific new meaning. Refers now to housing developed under the old development arrangements, with low rents that are set according to a government formula.
Tenant Services Authority (TSA)	The current regulator for housing associations and other social landlords. Created the new co-regulation framework, with the National Standards and the 'local offer'. To be abolished from April 2012, with its responsibilities passing to the HCA.

Finding out more

Housing jargon: 7th edition, National Housing Federation, 2010 – a comprehensive and updated decoder of jargon and acronyms used in social housing and related fields.

A2   Board member responsibilities at a glance

Here is a summary, in everyday language, of the main duties and responsibilities of a board member of a housing association or other social landlord.

In brief

Board members need to work as a team to:

- Set out the vision for the organisation, define its values, mission and overall direction, then protect and uphold these

- Make sure there are strategies and plans in place to deliver the objects set out in the organisation's governing document, and that they are being delivered effectively

- Make sure the organisation complies with its own governing document, and all the laws and regulations that apply to it.

In more detail

Leadership – board members have ultimate responsibility for directing the affairs of the organisation and ensuring that it is solvent, well-run and delivering the outcomes for which it has been set up.

Compliance and integrity – board members must:

- make sure the organisation complies (as required by its status) with company law, industrial and provident society law, and/or charity law, also with the requirements of the social housing regulator;

- ensure that the organisation complies with its own governing document and remains true to its purpose and objects;

- comply with the requirements of all the legislation and other regulators (if any) that govern the organisation's activities;

- act with integrity and avoid any personal conflicts of interest or misuse of the organisation's funds or assets.

Prudence – board members must:

- ensure that the organisation is and will remain solvent;

- use funds and assets reasonably and only in furtherance of the organisation's objects as set out in its governing document;

- avoid undertaking activities that might place the organisation's funds, assets or reputation at undue risk;

- take special care when borrowing funds or investing funds.

Duty of care – board members must:

- use reasonable skill and care in their work as board members, using their personal skills and experience as needed, to ensure that the organisation is well-run and efficient;

- consider getting external professional advice on all matters where there may be a material risk to the organisation, or where board members may be in breach of their duties.

A3   The housing association framework
In brief

Housing associations and other types of social landlord are independent, not-for-profit social businesses set up with a mission to provide affordable homes for people in housing need. They are run by boards which are primarily non-executive. The majority of board members are unpaid volunteers, although the board members of some associations now receive payment. Housing associations and other social landlords currently provide over 2.5m homes for more than 5m people in England. The vast majority of these households have limited housing options and do not have the choices that are available to people with higher incomes. Associations charge below market rents that are 'affordable' by people on low incomes. The government helps make this possible by providing subsidies from the taxpayer, either as capital grants, or through housing benefit to help tenants pay their rent.

Housing associations work in partnership with local authorities to help meet local housing needs. Many also offer opportunities for low-cost home ownership. Some offer support for people with a range of needs, including older people, people with disabilities and learning difficulties, and people who have been homeless. Many are also involved in community initiatives such as employment training, regeneration and projects with children and young people.

The Tenant Services Authority (TSA) currently supervises and regulates the activities of housing associations that receive public funding. The Homes and Communities Agency (HCA) provides capital grants for new homes and regeneration, and will also take responsibility for regulation from April 2012, when the TSA will cease to operate. It is also proposed that by this time the HCA's powers will be transferred to the Greater London Authority in that area. The Housing Ombudsman provides redress for tenant complaints.

In more detail

Legislation

There is no legal definition for a 'housing association'. The Housing and Regeneration Act 2008 requires all housing associations and other social housing providers that have received, or wish to be eligible to receive, public funds to register with the Tenant Services Authority as registered providers. The TSA sets standards and has a range of powers to compel registered providers to comply with them. The Government has proposed that this role focuses only on serious failures rather than proactive monitoring in the future.

Housing associations must also comply with the legislation that applies to their form of incorporation and the activities that the organisation undertakes. Aside from general charity, company, housing and construction legislation, this will include legislation covering employment, health and safety, equality and, if applicable, other areas such as protection for children and vulnerable people. European legislation also plays an increasing role (for instance in relation to procurement).

Corporate bodies

Housing associations have a range of different forms of legal status:

- About one-third are 'exempt charities' that have charitable status but are registered as industrial and provident societies with the registrar (currently the Financial Services Authority) rather than the Charity Commission (usually under the National Housing Federation's model rules)

- Another third are charities registered with the Charity Commission, either operating under trust deeds or as companies limited by guarantee

- The balance are non-charities also registered as industrial and provident societies with the FSA (usually under Federation model rules)

- A small but growing number are companies limited by guarantee that do not trade for profit (the Housing Act 1996 enabled not-for-profit housing companies to become eligible for registration without having to be charities).

Every housing association has a governing document (often called 'the rules') that defines its objectives and sets out detailed procedures that it must follow. The nature of the governing document depends on the legal status of the organisation. The rules define the activities that the organisation can carry out and the powers of the board. Most rules have a number of common features and purposes which include:

- defining its social mission or purposes;

- defining the status of members and how they are admitted;

- the size and role of the board and how it is elected;

- appointment of the chair and secretary;

- the conduct of board meetings;

- the conduct of the annual and other general meetings;

- establishing committees;

- powers to borrow and invest;

- audit and accounting requirements; and

- amendment of the rules.

There are variations of non-charitable rules for a range of different housing associations from co-operatives to large scale voluntary transfer associations (LSVTs). In the case of housing organisations set up to take the transfer of local authority housing, it is likely that the rules will include some formal provisions about the continuing role of the local authority. This might include the ability to nominate board members, and the ability to veto certain changes to the rules.

Rules periodically need to be reviewed and updated. Major revisions to Federation model rules are made from time to time. The 'plain English' version introduced in 1996 and revised in

2000, 2005 and 2011 has reflected the many changes that resulted from the National Housing Federation's Code of governance. It is worth making sure that your organisation's rules are up-to-date. The Federation provides advice on this for its members.

Shareholding members

The rules of industrial and provident societies and the memorandum and articles of companies limited by guarantee provide for shareholding members whose primary responsibility is to elect the board. In some cases, shareholders are referred to as 'guarantors', but their function is the same.

Shareholding members have the power – at a general meeting – to appoint the auditors, amend the rules, appoint and remove board members and approve or reject mergers. This gives them a measure of control that, at times, can be crucial. However, the board usually determines who can become a shareholder and so there is an element of circularity in the accountability of the board to the members of the association or company. Associations and companies should have a clear policy on shareholding membership.

The role of the regulators

The Tenant Services Authority took over from the Housing Corporation as the regulator of social housing in April 2009. The TSA has three main aims:

- a fair deal for tenants;

- to ensure providers are financially viable, efficient and well run (to protect taxpayer and private investment); and

- to encourage the supply of new housing.

One of the TSA's achievements has been the introduction of a different approach to monitoring standards called 'co-regulation': landlords and tenants work together to improve services within a framework of six National Standards.

Housing associations seeking capital funding also have to comply with the requirements of the Homes and Communities Agency.

Until recently, housing associations with more than 1,000 homes were inspected on a periodic basis by the Audit Commission. Inspections focused particularly on service delivery outcomes as experienced by tenants, leaseholders and other service users.

The Government has announced plans to abolish the Audit Commission and to make the TSA a statutory committee of the HCA. It is likely that the new co-regulatory approach will continue, but with a stronger focus on financial viability and value for money for the taxpayer. 'Backstop' consumer regulation will concentrate on setting clear standards and addressing serious failures, with inspections only where serious failure is suspected. An enhanced ombudsman service will pick up and remedy poor service.

Depending on their precise legal status, housing associations are also subject to a degree of regulation by the Financial Services Authority. Housing associations providing housing with high levels of support may come within the scope of the Care Quality Commission.

Housing associations which are charities

Housing associations which are registered charities must follow Charity Commission guidance on issues relating to their charitable status, including submitting annual returns and accounts, and may need additional consents when disposing of property assets.

Finding out more

The regulatory framework for social housing in England from April 2010. Tenant Services Authority, 2010.

A guide to the Housing and Regeneration Act 2008. National Housing Federation, 2008.

Model rules. National Housing Federation, 2011.

Governance...the small print: A range of model governance documents covering key policy areas (2nd Edition). National Housing Federation, 2008.

Companies Act 2006.

Industrial and Provident Societies Acts 1965 and 1968.

Charities Act 2006

Excellence in governance: Code for members and good practice guidance. National Housing Federation, revised edition, 2010.

A4 How to use this book

This book is intended as a practical handbook for board members who are new to the role, and as a useful refresher for board members with greater experience. Each chapter looks at a different aspect of the role and provides a brief answer to your most likely questions. Each answer is accompanied by a more detailed explanation for those who want it.

- For an explanation of the board's role and responsibilities, see Chapter B

- For guidance on your role and responsibilities, see Chapter C

- For the main aspects of running the business, see Chapter D

- For relationships with outside parties and organisations, see Chapter E

- For responsibilities as a landlord, see Chapter F

- For how to work with tenants, see Chapter G

- For property matters, see Chapter H

- For responsibilities as an employer, see Chapter J.

A5 The ever-changing world of housing
The growth of the housing association movement

The housing association movement has its origins in medieval almshouses. Victorian philanthropy gave it a major impetus. A further big expansion took place in the 1960s and early 1970s, principally as a reaction to unscrupulous private landlords and widespread slum clearance.

The Housing Act 1974 was decisive in launching the modern housing association movement. It brought in the system of Housing Association Grant (now Social Housing Grant or SHG) that has remained ever since. It established a regulatory framework and led to a dramatic expansion of government funding for housing associations.

In 1981, in line with its policy to encourage home ownership, the government introduced the right to buy at a discount for tenants of non-charitable associations and local authorities. Opportunities for low cost home ownership and shared ownership came into being at the same time.

The Housing Act 1988 ushered in the era of private finance. Alongside greater freedom to set rents, associations now had to raise the balance of costs from the private sector and take all the development risks. Associations were also encouraged to be more entrepreneurial, which has led to occasional difficulties for those which did not properly manage the risks involved. Transfer of local authority homes to housing associations also began at this time, providing a major boost to the sector.

More recently, the Housing and Regeneration Act 2008 created the TSA and the HCA, and opened the way towards a mixed economy of social housing, with housing associations, local authorities, arm's length management organisations (ALMOs) and the private sector all having a role. The Localism Bill 2011 (when enacted) will make further changes, bringing the TSA and HCA back together again, and heralding a new system for development, based on 'affordable rents' set at 80 per cent of market levels.

Housing associations have responded to housing needs in many different ways over the years. The result is a rich diversity of organisation. The smallest have only a few properties and no paid staff, while the largest have more than 50,000 properties and employ thousands of staff. Some work in a small geographical area while others are regional or national in their scope. Some meet a very wide range of needs while others have a much tighter focus. Of the 1,500+ associations currently registered with the TSA, one-third have no staff. On the other hand, the 25 largest associations manage about 27 per cent of the sector's stock and employ thousands of staff. In short, there is no such thing as a typical housing association.

Housing associations are increasingly expected to be innovative community leaders as well as excellent service providers. Tenant and local empowerment needs to be at the heart of their activities, as must a focus on the provision of excellent and improving services.

Continuing pressure from the government to secure economies of scale in the procurement of new housing and to make better use of the assets and surpluses that associations generate has concentrated capital funding into significantly fewer hands and encouraged consolidation of the sector.

Local authorities

Local authorities dominated social housing provision until the 1980s. Then the right to buy significantly reduced their stock. Government funding for new homes ceased and housing associations became the main providers of new grant-aided homes at below market rents. Transfers of stock to newly established associations further reduced the number of local authority homes.

While housing associations have enjoyed greater access to government grants for housing development, it is local authorities that have statutory housing responsibilities and direct accountability to the local electorate. Housing associations work closely with local authorities in many aspects of their work. Nominations of prospective tenants continue to be a key resource to local authorities. In many areas, there are now common waiting lists and joint approaches to local housing problems.

Today local authorities in England own about 2m homes, of which about half are managed by ALMOs (autonomous but local authority-owned management companies). While most local authority housing has been modernised, pressing needs still remain. The need to deliver Decent Homes invites competition for housing funds but also provides opportunities for collaboration and joint working. The ability of housing associations to raise private finance outside the public sector borrowing requirement gives them an additional ability to make public grants go further. This has been an important incentive for local authorities to transfer their stock to housing associations.

Local authorities now take a more strategic approach to the housing requirements of everyone in their communities, not just the households living in social housing. They also help set the HCA's priorities in their area for new investment.

Demand

A number of reports over the last 10 years have highlighted the difference between the demand for and supply of social rented housing. The need for decent rented housing is no less pressing. In areas of high property values, those on average incomes cannot afford to buy their home and this has caused acute housing problems for teachers, National Health Service (NHS) staff and other workers. Many housing waiting lists have lengthened; the numbers in bed-and-breakfast accommodation or other temporary housing solutions run into thousands.

The need for investment is complicated by the changing regional pattern of demand for housing. In some areas of the country (particularly, but not exclusively, in parts of the North) there is an excess of rented housing. This can make properties hard to let and contributes to pockets of economic decline. In other parts of the country (particularly the South East) demand for social housing far outstrips supply. However, this makes housing provision more expensive and adds great pressures to areas of scarce green space.

Meeting tenants' full range of needs

Meeting tenants' needs in responsive and sensitive ways is a constant challenge for all housing associations. The introduction of the TSA National Standards and co-regulation placed a spotlight on the quality of services to tenants and leaseholders. While customer care techniques are undoubtedly useful, housing associations need to remember that, from their tenants' perspective, they are monopoly suppliers.

Changes are also taking place in the way people live. There is a long-established trend towards smaller households. The number of people living alone is growing and people are living longer. The numbers of older people are rising sharply and the numbers of very old people (over 85) are expected to double over the next 10 years. There will be a growing need for appropriate housing and support. It also means that the proportion of the total population that is economically active is declining. Family stability has declined. In addition to family break-ups causing an increase in smaller households, there is greater fluidity as families form and re-form as relationships change; matching appropriately sized social housing to needs becomes more difficult.

Personalisation of care and support

Many housing associations provide additional support to some of their tenants (often in conjunction with specialist care agencies), and some specialise in combining housing and support for people with a range of disabilities or special needs.

The main responsibility for revenue funding of care and support services rests with local authorities. In recent years there have been major efforts to encourage and support independent living and provide care that is tailored to an individual's needs rather than fit individuals to the requirements of bureaucratic services and institutions. At the same time, the funding of care has moved increasingly from revenue support of schemes to support for individuals. The main funding stream is known as Supporting People, and this is currently being reduced as part of wider spending cuts.

The latest initiative is a cross-government vision to transform adult social care known as 'personalisation'. It is designed to increase individual choice and control, and to encourage a strategic shift towards prevention and keeping people well instead of just dealing with crisis situations. Increasingly, individuals will have access to personal budgets and personal payments to purchase their own support. This is likely to lead to fundamental changes in the way in which care and support services are provided.

Danger of concentrating poverty

Large-scale building programmes have led to the development of many large housing estates. Important lessons have been learnt from the earlier experiences of local housing authorities. Large, poorly designed estates without adequate community facilities can become very unpop-ular with tenants, and encourage a downward spiral of crime and vandalism. But the pressures that led to the search for large-scale solutions remain. Some housing associations have built large estates and others will acquire them through stock transfers. The pressure to reduce the

costs of additional housing has led to an increase in new build schemes at the expense of rehabilitation, and to larger developments away from town and city centres. This has also led to the
deterioration of many inner city residential areas and encouraged the flight to the suburbs. The
needs of urban regeneration can therefore conflict with other economic priorities.

The difficulties in tackling concentrations of poverty, unemployment and poor housing are now
better understood. There is a clearer understanding that a combination of benefit dependency,
unemployment and poor local facilities can leave people feeling that they are excluded from
society. This combination of factors also provides a common backdrop to a prevalent drugs
sub-culture. Pouring money into new housing is not enough. Indeed, it can be counter-
productive if the results are even higher concentrations of benefit dependency.

Regeneration has to take account of schools, health, crime, shops, jobs and all the other
facilities that make an area attractive. Only if these are tackled systematically is the result
likely to be sustainable. Housing may only play a modest part in an area regeneration proposal.
Housing associations and companies will have to work in partnership with others if they are to
be effective in tackling regeneration.

Pressure on public expenditure

The level of national debt is high. The proportion of the population that is economically active
and that is most associated with generating wealth is declining. The number of retired people is
increasing sharply and young people are staying longer in some form of education or training.
Unemployment remains at significant levels. At the same time, expectations and costs of health
care and education are rising, as is the cost of state pensions and other benefits. These factors
combine to put the government under severe public expenditure constraints, and cuts are being
implemented in most of the public sector.

Whether the housing sector continues to make a growing contribution to meeting housing
needs depends on the level of resources that the government is able to make available, as well
as on the innovation and energy of housing associations. In recent years, housing has not been
near the top of the list of spending priorities, and the coalition government has reduced the
amount of grant available.

Rents have risen substantially faster than inflation since the mid-1980s. As a result, the cost of
support to those who cannot afford to pay their rents (mainly in the form of housing benefit)
has also risen sharply. The increasing cost of housing benefit to the government has led to
proposals to limit eligibility and set upper limits on what can be claimed.

The challenge to meet needs is as urgent as ever, and growing. And the government's requirement to limit public expenditure means that there are constant pressures to do more for less, to reduce costs and to become more efficient.

A6   Why become a board member?

Whatever the size of housing association, and whatever your particular skills and experience, being a board member is an opportunity to help meet social housing needs. You will help to shape your organisation's particular contribution and join with others in coping with the changes, problems and opportunities that this involves. At a time when so many people feel increasingly powerless, this is an opportunity to make a difference, and to offer a valued social contribution.

The management of a housing association requires a range of different skills and experience. This may include understanding of the needs that your organisation is particularly trying to address. Or it may be that you can contribute with knowledge of one or more of the following areas:

- community contacts and activity;

- provision of housing or other services;

- asset management and development;

- financial and treasury management;

- business or professional experience;

- experience as a tenant; or

- other skills relevant to your particular organisation.

Whatever your background, your willingness to put effort into the role, work productively and share responsibility with your colleagues will be crucial. So, too, will your common sense, whiich is, as we all know, not that common.

Being a board member is likely to develop your skills and broaden your experience. You will learn from the skills and experience that others bring as well as contributing your own. Taking all these factors together, the job of being the board member of a housing association or housing company can bring personal satisfaction and fulfilment. There will be occasions when you may grudge the time, or when difficult decisions need to be taken. Being a board member is never easy. But playing a part in a successful social enterprise is both interesting and worthwhile.

Chapter B

_____

The work of the board

Excellent service delivery depends on good governance, financial strength and value for money. As standards of governance have evolved, greater expectations have been put on board members as a consequence. It is very much in the interests of housing associations to be at the forefront of best practice.

The regulatory regime unambiguously makes boards responsible for meeting the National Standards and delivering excellent and responsive services to tenants.

Housing associations have many reasons for being open and accountable. They enjoy the privilege of substantial public funding and are close to a monopoly position in the provision of new subsidised housing. They provide a key community service to people who have relatively little freedom of choice. They are the largest providers of social housing in the country. All these factors make accountability and openness a central requirement for housing associations.

B1 What is good governance?

In brief

'Governance' is an all-encompassing term for organisational leadership, direction, control and accountability. Its function is to ensure that an organisation fulfils its overall purpose, achieves its intended outcomes, and operates in an effective, efficient and ethical manner. In recent years there has been concern about standards of corporate behaviour. The National Housing Federation has taken a lead in setting governance standards for its members.

The foundation of good governance is having a board that is balanced, diverse and effective, which leads and controls the organisation and complies with its legal requirements.

In more detail

Excellence in governance: Code for members and good practice guidance

The National Housing Federation Code of governance is designed to support Federation members in being excellent at governing their organisations and being accountable, independent and diverse. First published in 1995 and most recently revised in 2010, the code has been widely acclaimed as an example of best practice.

The code is based on nine principles of good governance and sets out a main principle and specific provisions for each of 12 key aspects of board behaviour and approach. Housing associations are expected to put the code into practice in a way that is appropriate to their size and profile, and to provide explanations about any areas where they do not comply. The code also contains extensive good practice guidance.

Other codes

The *UK Corporate Governance Code* sets out principles of good governance for public companies listed on the London Stock Exchange. Originally produced in 1992, and most recently revised in 2010, it is designed to address concerns about standards of corporate behaviour.

In 2004, the Independent Commission for Good Governance in Public Services chaired by Sir Alan Langlands published *The Good Governance Standard for Public Services* as a guide for all organisations providing publicly funded services. The Standard builds on the Nolan principles for the conduct of individuals in public life (selflessness, integrity, objectivity, accountability, openness, honesty and leadership) and sets out six core principles of good governance.

In 2005, a group of voluntary sector bodies and the Charity Commission published *Good Governance: A Code for the Voluntary and Community Sector* (subsequently revised in 2010) to help voluntary board members and charity trustees carry out their work. The code sets out seven principles of good governance for boards to follow.

Putting it into practice

Good governance requires:

- clarity about the structure and the distinct roles of the key parties (board, chief executive, chair etc.) and developing their capacity to be effective;

- a focus on the organisation's purpose and outcomes for tenants and service users;

- an ethos that demonstrates values and ethics through high standards of conduct and behaviour;

- capacity to perform effectively, take informed and transparent decisions and manage risk; and

- real engagement with, and accountability to, tenants and other stakeholders.

This handbook is a guide for board members on putting good governance into practice. The board will only be effective in its many roles and responsibilities if it maintains its own strength and performance. This begins with having the right balance of skills and experience. Depending on the particular focus of the organisation's work, the board is likely to need experience and understanding of all or most of the following:

- working as an effective team to take strategic decisions for social result;

- direct knowledge of the needs and aspirations of the communities and people served;

- general business, financial and management skills;

- the external framework and operating environment for Federation members; and

- other relevant skills, such as human resources, legal, property and development, and public affairs.

The board should include people with managerial experience of organisations at least as large as the housing association. It should try and avoid dependence on any one person for a key skill. The board should also seek a reasonable gender and age balance. Where it serves diverse communities, it is particularly important that those communities are represented on the board so that it understands their distinctive needs and views. No board is likely to have a perfect mix. Common sense, training and commitment are all crucial ingredients.

Finding out more

Excellence in governance: Code for members and good practice guidance. Revised edition 2010; and *Excellence in governance: compliance checklist.* National Housing Federation, 2010.

The UK Corporate Governance Code. Financial Reporting Council, 2010. www.frc.org.uk.

The Good Governance Standard for Public Services. Independent Commission for Good Governance in Public Services, chaired by Sir Alan Langlands. OPM and CIPFA, 2004: www.opm.co.uk.

Good Governance: A Code for the Voluntary and Community Sector. The Code Founding Group, 2010: www.ncvo-vol.org.uk/codeofgovernance.

B2   What is the board's job?

In brief

The board's job is to lead and control the organisation, set its direction and act wholly in its best interests. Except in the smallest organisations with no staff, the board does not manage the day-to-day work, which is delegated to the chief executive and other staff.

In more detail

The board's role

The purpose of the board is to determine strategy, direct, control, scrutinise and evaluate an organisation's affairs. Key aspects of the board's role are:

- **Guarding the purpose**: the board determines the focus of a housing association's work. As external circumstances change, the organisation's objectives have to be reconciled with what is practicable and achievable without compromising the association's core purpose and core values.

- **Setting strategic direction, plans and objectives**: the wider objectives of the housing association are only likely to be achieved if they are translated into clear plans and strategies.

- **Setting high standards of conduct and probity**: the board must behave with high standards of probity and integrity, and ensure that these apply throughout the organisation, so as to ensure continuing public support.

- **Setting the delegation framework**: clarity of delegation helps to achieve a clear and effective relationship with staff and is an essential safeguard for the board. The board should spell out which decisions are reserved for the board and then clearly delegate the rest.

- **Taking key decisions**: some decisions will always be of such importance that they should only be taken by the board, for example, a substantial change in direction or where substantial financial or reputational risks are at issue.

- **Financial control and managing risk**: almost anything that helps the association to achieve its objectives will involve risk. The board has an overriding responsibility for the financial viability of the organisation and for managing risk.

- **Scrutinising performance and holding the executive to account**: having set clear strategies and plans and a clear framework of delegation, the board must scrutinise performance and check that work is progressing as intended and objectives are being achieved. And if not, take appropriate remedial action.

- **Appointing and remunerating the chief executive**: for housing associations employing staff, the appointment of the chief executive is one of the most important decisions that the board has to take.

- **Ensuring accountability**: the board needs to ensure that tenants and other stakeholders can monitor the organisation's performance and hold the board to account.

Board role in large housing associations

In larger and more complex housing associations, the board will concentrate on broader issues of strategy and policy and overall performance monitoring. The overall volume of activity will make it less appropriate for board members to get involved in issues of detail. Large organisations tend to employ more staff, including experienced senior managers. There will generally be a higher level of delegation to staff through the chief executive. Experience of how large organisations work will be particularly relevant for some board members.

Board role in smaller housing associations

With fewer funds and staff at their disposal than larger organisations, smaller housing associations have to be resourceful in how they deliver their services and in how they manage their day-to-day work. In very small associations, the board has to get more involved in managerial issues and cannot just direct operations. What makes this practical is the smaller scale of the organisation's work. Some board members will need to have practical experience of the main functions of the organisation.

Board role in housing associations with no staff

One-third of all housing associations registered with the Tenant Services Authority (as registered providers) have no staff. These will generally be smaller housing associations, or charities such as almshouses and Abbeyfield Societies. Either board members and other volunteers carry out the day-to-day work or it is carried out by agents (often other housing associations). Where the work is carried out by board members, it is necessary for members to make a distinction between their individual tasks and their collective role as board members. It is particularly important that the extent of delegation to individual members is set out in writing.

The use of other housing associations as agents can help the board. However, there is always a danger of conflicting priorities and the agent will often be a much larger organisation. Agency agreements are essential and should include clear arrangements for:

- all the services that are to be provided;

- standards of performance;

- monitoring performance;

- payment.

Finding out more

Read through the terms of reference for your board. if you are a board member in a group structure, you may wish also to read through the intra-group agreement.

B3   How does the board work as a team?

In brief

Board members share a collective responsibility for everything that the board does and need to work together collaboratively as a team. Like any other team, the board will only be effective if it is pulling in the same direction and can resolve differences of opinion amicably. A board has a right to expect that all its members will support the organisation's objectives and policies once these have been agreed.

In more detail

Working together

All members share a responsibility for working with the chair and with each other to make decisions and deal with the business smoothly and effectively in the time available. Working together collaboratively and effectively is often a challenge when members only meet each other from time to time, and particularly for members who are new. To maximise performance and effectiveness, the board will need to ensure that:

- members are clear about their role and new members receive good induction to get up to speed quickly;

- good servicing which enables members to conduct board business efficiently and make best use of the time spent together in meetings;

- members take regular opportunities away from the pressure of board business to plan longer term; and

- performance appraisal and renewal take place regularly, so as to ensure that the board performs to best effect and recruits and retains the right mix of members.

Effective support and servicing

Effective board meetings rely heavily on effective servicing. This is not just a matter of ensuring that board papers are provided in time. The structure of the agenda also plays a key role. There is no single best way of servicing the board. Many have found the following practices helpful:

- the order of business is agreed in advance with the chair and the treatment of difficult or contentious matters discussed beforehand;

- board papers are circulated at least one week in advance and no late papers tabled (other than in the most exceptional circumstances);

- being able to produce clear and concise papers is part of the appraisal criteria for all senior managers;

- items for decision or consultation are kept separate from items for information only;

- items of strategy, policies and procedures and key decisions are grouped and come before less important business;

- reports from committees are treated as items for information unless there is a specific recommendation to be considered;

- the chair timetables the agenda items in line with the board's wishes for the overall duration for the meeting; and

- minutes are cleared by the chair prior to circulation.

There are many other ingredients that will help make sure board meetings are effective. Is the meeting frequency appropriate for dealing with the business? Does the time and place suit as many members as possible? Is the location accessible? Are refreshments provided? Is help available for transport or child care? If there are other practical ways that will help the board work together as a team, suggest them.

Awaydays and strategy forums

Many boards find it very difficult to stand back and take a strategic perspective in busy board meetings. Awaydays (or weekend seminars) allow time for more considered discussion away from the pressure of dealing with immediate business. They are particularly useful for the board and senior managers to:

- team build and develop better working relationships;

- look further into the future than is possible during a board meeting;

- discuss and develop strategies and plans;

- consider major new policy directions or other major issues;

- undertake SWOT (strengths, weaknesses, opportunities and threats) and PESTLE (political, economic, social and technical, legal and environmental) analyses; and

- appraise the effectiveness of the board and committees (without staff present).

In the last few years, some boards have opted to vary their governance 'menu' by alternating board meetings with strategy forums that allow for more in-depth discussion of issues.

Board appraisal

Taking time to reflect on how well the board deals with its business and how well members are working together helps to maintain board effectiveness and ensures that the board adds maximum value to the work of the housing association. The board should have formal mechanisms for assessing its own effectiveness and the performance of individual members and the chair. At the least there should be an annual discussion without the pressure of other board business. Every two years, it is good practice for this review to involve an independent perspective. This makes it harder for complacency to set in.

Renewal

Achieving the right balance of skills does not happen by accident or chance election. The board should periodically take stock of its composition and seek to redress any imbalances or skills shortages. New members should be recruited on a systematic and open basis, rather than just through friends of friends. This can probably best be achieved by delegating the recruitment process to a nominations committee. The board should publish its policy and process for selecting new members. Gradual renewal is preferable to wider changes at infrequent intervals. This also helps to keep the board lively and open to new ideas. Renewal is underpinned by setting a maximum number of years that a board member can serve. The National Housing Federation's Code of governance sets this at a maximum of nine years.

Finding out more

Achieving excellence: Board appraisal, Ann Gibson. National Housing Federation, 2007.

Familiarise yourself with your board's approach to team, individual and chair appraisal.

B4 How is the board accountable?
In brief

The board has a duty to be open and accountable for the organisation's work and performance, and for compliance with the law and good practice.

Housing associations have a range of accountabilities: to tenants and other customers, to local authorities, to funders, to the regulator and to the wider community. Real accountability involves more than just giving an account of, and being held to account for, the organisation's actions and performance. It also means welcoming and being responsive to feedback, and taking account of the requirements and views of tenants and other stakeholders in the planning and provision of services.

In more detail

The National Housing Federation Code of service delivery and accountability

In 2006 the Tenant Involvement Commission looked at what housing association tenants want. Its report *What Tenants Want* made four main recommendations:

- get the basics right and go the extra mile – be a good landlord before you do anything else (the wider community is important but not as important as the basics);

- provide choice;

- make involvement personal; and

- be accountable.

The Commission also recommended that associations introduce a service and accountability pledge and a code of tenant involvement. In response, the National Housing Federation introduced *Excellence in service delivery and accountability: Code for members*, as a commitment to excellence and a promise to be open and accountable. The code is designed to support members in understanding their residents' needs and expectations and delivering the highest possible standards of customer service within the resources available, based on real and effective engagement with local people and meaningful choice. For examples of how housing associations are implementing the code, see www.housing.org.uk/customerfocus.

Tenants, residents and customers

Tenants (as well as leaseholders, shared owners, licensees and other residents) are the principal recipients of housing association services and have the greatest interest in ensuring that services are excellent and cost-effective, and also that they are sensitive to the full range of tenants' needs. Most tenants have few choices about where they live and little scope to take their custom elsewhere, unless they live in areas of low demand (in which case they may well face other problems). Accountability to tenants requires comprehensive and systematic arrangements for ensuring that tenants are consulted about the way the housing association provides its services, and that their voices are heard and taken into account on the issues that concern them (not always the same thing).

Tenant board members help the board to be aware of the impact of its decisions on tenants, and contribute to open decision-making. Individual tenants can also bring other competencies and experience as effective board members. There should be no such thing as 'tenant board members', but just board members who are tenants. Having tenant board members does not create accountability to tenants as a whole. Even where there are formal structures for tenant representatives to be elected to the board, there is still a need to have tenant consultation arrangements that are accessible to all tenants. This requires many mechanisms that suit the circumstances of individual tenants. These are best developed with tenants for tenants rather than being imposed by the board. It is also the role of the whole board to care about how the tenant voice is heard.

Local authorities

Local authorities have both a strategic housing function and statutory housing responsibilities. They derive their accountability from the local electorate. Most housing associations work in partnership with local authorities and contribute to meeting housing need and creating sustainable communities. The board should ensure that the association maintains constructive relationships with the main local authorities in whose areas the organisation works.

Where an organisation has a substantial presence and is a key provider, it should seek to establish clear arrangements for regular consultation on key matters of mutual interest (if appropriate, backed up by written agreements) including allocations and lettings (often a common or unified approach); nominations; annual information to be published; and housing benefit payment.

Funders and lenders

The benefits of substantial public subsidy place a duty on registered providers to be accountable, through grant providers, to Parliament and to the wider public whose taxes fund the grants. This accountability is mainly exercised through the overall regulation of the Tenant Services Authority and the detailed procedures that must be observed for obtaining grant.

Accountability to lenders is contractual through loan agreements which usually contain formal reporting requirements. However, it is a good idea to maintain an ongoing dialogue and to alert lenders in advance if any potential difficulties are foreseen. Providing boards act prudently and reasonably, lenders are usually also reasonable.

The regulators and inspectors

Accountability to regulators and inspectors is the main way that the government and the public hold housing associations to account for their performance. Regulation is an essential feature of providing core services to the community with the benefit of public funds. It is also a protection for the key role that housing associations play in delivering social housing. Public subsidy rests ultimately on public consent. Individual tenants also have rights of redress through the Housing Ombudsman.

The wider community

Accountability to the wider community requires openness of information and a willingness to admit and correct mistakes when they arise. The board must set the tone for this openness and encourage it at all levels.

Housing associations can have a major impact on the communities in which they operate. Major developments can disrupt existing communities. Unless carefully planned, they can also create unbalanced communities with inadequate facilities. The board should ensure that arrangements are made to take account of community views. Organisations that are major providers in an area also have a duty to work constructively with other agencies.

It is difficult for organisations with a wide geographical spread to be sensitive to local communities. Distance and inaccessibility can be serious blocks to effective local accountability. It is widely regarded as good practice for the boards of such organisations to establish regional or area committees that can relate more effectively to local communities.

Accountability to shareholding members

The boards of most traditional housing associations are elected by the organisation's shareholding members. However, the impact of accountability to shareholding members is limited as most housing associations have few members (in many cases comprising mainly present and past board members). Accountability is usually also circular as it is the board that decides who can become a member.

The board has the responsibility for developing the organisation's membership policy. This should be geared to helping the organisation meet its objectives by:

- strengthening relationships with stakeholders;

- balancing different interests;

- maintaining constitutional stability.

In the case of transfer associations and companies, the shareholding arrangements are likely to be organised into three constituencies that balance the interests of residents, the local authority and independent members. Board members may be nominated (in the case of the local authority) or directly elected by all residents (in the case of resident representatives). Only the independent board members may be elected by other shareholders. In larger groups, some or all board members may be appointed by the 'parent' of the group.

Finding out more

Excellence in service delivery and accountability: Code for members. National Housing Federation, 2009

What Tenants Want: Report of the Tenant Involvement Commission. National Housing Federation, 2006: www.housing.org.uk.

B5 What do committees of the board do?

In brief

Committees provide expertise and help the board to scrutinise performance, deliver effective corporate governance and manage risk. Committees allow a more in-depth focus on particular aspects of the board's work than is possible in board meetings. They are able to go into issues in greater detail and can provide opportunities for detailed scrutiny of performance and other matters.

However, overly complex committee structures can lead to duplication and fragmentation of the board's efforts, delays in decision-making and a consequent loss of cohesion. They can also take up a disproportionate amount of senior management time on committee servicing rather than on taking forward the organisation's work. Boards should ensure that the organisational structure is kept as simple as possible and that its value is worth the time and resources invested in it.

In more detail

What committees do

Many housing associations, particularly the larger ones, have committees (sometimes called subcommittees) established by the board for various purposes. Some also have separate subsidiaries which will have their own boards (see next section). Boards that have established committees usually expect most board members to also be a member of one or more committee.

There is no ideal model for committees of the board. For many years, the most common committee structure was to have functional committees matching the main functions of the organisation. These were typically: finance, housing services and development. Other committees might oversee the selection of board members, senior staff salaries, audit etc. There is usually a trade-off between the ability to give a more detailed look at functional areas and the frequency of board meetings. The result is that, where there are committees, there is usually a set cycle of committee meetings followed by a board meeting. Often the cycle is quarterly or bi-monthly.

The interdependence of many issues, which can mean that matters are frequently discussed at two or even more committees before coming to the board, has led many organisations to reduce the number of committees. There is a trend towards some of the functions being combined or retained by the board, and the board meeting more frequently (eg, six-weekly to every two months).

Being on a committee but not the board

It is common for committees of the board to have some members who are board members and some who are not. This flexibility enables the committee to recruit particular experience, such as tenants and residents, or particular expertise, for example, development or finance. A committee member who is not a board member will have fewer responsibilities than one who is. The responsibilities of individual committee members should be defined in writing in addition to the committee's terms of reference. Some prospective board members may serve on a committee prior to their appointment to the main board.

Audit and risk

The board can discharge its internal control responsibilities more effectively by establishing an audit committee or by ensuring that another committee discharges the functions of an audit committee. The audit committee (or equivalent) should have an overview of:

- financial reporting;

- internal control and risk management systems;

- compliance, whistle blowing and fraud;

- internal audit; and

- external audit.

It is regarded as good practice for larger associations to have an audit committee, the members of which should all be non-executives and not include the chair.

The board is responsible for determining the nature and extent of the significant risks it is willing to take in achieving its strategic objectives. There are occasions on which it may be more appropriate for risk to be monitored closely by committee, most commonly in some form of combination of risk and audit.

Finance

Financial control affects every area of work. It measures the organisation's effectiveness as well as the resources that are available to meet its objectives, and is crucial in an operating framework that requires housing associations to manage their own risks. It is as important for a not-for-profit organisation as for any other type of business. While overall financial control is a board responsibility, a finance committee can bring a sharper focus to the task. A typical finance committee's remit is to:

- oversee the organisation's financial affairs;

- ensure the organisation remains solvent;

- ensure the organisation has appropriate financial policies and control mechanisms in place;

- ensure the chief executive maintains and implements financial procedures to protect the organisation's financial integrity and that officers keep proper books and records;

- review the management accounts, cash flow and budgets and make recommendations to the board as required; and

- review areas of financial risk.

Operations

Operations usually encompasses all service-delivery-focused activities and may also include development and asset management. Typically, operations committees will:

- oversee the development and implementation of business plan objectives relating to service delivery;

- scrutinise the quality, performance and non-financial risk management of services (eg, housing and estate management, maintenance and asset management, community development, training and employment etc.);

- oversee the operating framework (quality system, continuous improvement, health and safety etc.);

- oversee arrangements for tenant involvement; and

- act as a sounding board for the chief executive and senior management on new developments and service improvements.

Some organisations, particularly those with developed area structures, may have a more narrowly focused performance committee, rather than an operations committee. More recently, a few have chosen to view the existence of a scrutiny panel as superseding that of a performance committee.

Development

Development poses particular risks and requires close scrutiny. Developing housing associations often have a development committee to oversee development on behalf of the board. Typically, development committees will be responsible for:

- development and procurement strategy;

- policy and delivery framework (design standards, scheme appraisal criteria, approach to procurement and tendering, consultant and contractor panels, level of delegation to staff, contaminated land policy etc.);

- key partnerships or schemes that pose particular risks (schemes above delegated authority, schemes with no grant funding etc.);

- monitoring implementation of the programme (allocation take-up, cash spend, scheme costs, tenant feedback, contractor and consultant performance etc.).

Governance, nominations and remuneration

Increasingly, housing associations have delegated arrangements for overseeing board performance and remuneration. Typically, such committees are responsible for:

- reviewing board structure, size and composition;

- board member recruitment and remuneration;

- appointment of the chair and senior independent director;

- remuneration of the chief executive and other senior executives;

- board and individual board member appraisal; and

- succession planning for board members and senior executives.

Members should all be non-executives and may include the chair as a member, but it is good practice for another committee member to chair the committee.

Human resources

Staff are a housing association's most valuable resource. A human resources committee can help the board fulfil its obligations relating to staffing, including recruitment, compensation, performance, succession, equality and diversity, and health and safety matters. A typical human resources committee will oversee:

- human resource (HR) management (strategy and policy for all matters relating to the recruitment, reward, retention, motivation and development of the association's staff);

- talent management (staff training, personal development, performance management, management development, HR aspects of organisational learning and knowledge etc.);

- employee relations (contracts of employment, staff handbooks, HR policies, disciplinary and grievance procedures, union recognition etc.);

- scrutiny of all staffing matters (training, sickness, turnover, reasons for leaving etc.);

- equality and diversity; and

- health and safety.

Area or regional committees

Larger organisations, particularly those associations with a wide geographical spread, may have area or regional committees. These may have a measure of responsibility for all of the organisation's operations in a defined area. Housing associations will not generally combine area committees with a full range of functional committees.

Ad hoc panels and working groups

Housing associations with a more streamlined committee structure often find it useful to establish time-limited joint working groups of staff and board members to work on a specific issue and prepare proposals for the board. This strengthens the partnership approach and avoids the bureaucracy of standing committees. A typical example might be a governance working group reviewing some of the governance processes or framework across an organisation or group of organisations.

Finding out more

ICSA Guidance on Terms of Reference – Audit Committee. ICSA, 2010: www. icsa.org.uk.

Guidance on Audit Committees. FRC, 2010: www.frc.gov.uk.

Audit Committees: Combined Code Guidance (the Smith Report). FRC, 2003: www.frc.gov.uk.

ICSA Guidance on Terms of Reference Nomination Committee. ICSA, 2010.

ICSA Guidance on Terms of Reference Remuneration Committee. ICSA, 2010.

Review of the role and effectiveness of non-executive directors (The Higgs Review). DTI, 2003: www.bis.gov.uk.

If you serve on a committee, read through the terms of reference.

B6 How do group structures work?

In brief

A 'group' is a combination of two or more organisations that work together and where one (the parent) has constitutional control of the others (the subsidiaries). Some groups have a dominant parent with subsidiaries that are, in effect, local business units. Other groups are more federal, with power and autonomy spread throughout the component organisations.

Group structures offer a flexible way for housing associations to structure their activities in different companies. But they also add significant layers of complexity to governance and can be time consuming and expensive to administer. Following changes in legislation that have relaxed restrictions on housing association activities, several groups have simplified their structures by amalgamating parent and subsidiary companies.

In more detail

Group structures

Most of the largest housing associations are part of housing groups, and groups now manage over 80 per cent of all housing association homes. Some parent organisations own no assets, while others may be the largest organisation within the group. Some groups include subsidiaries that are not registered with the Tenant Services Authority. In a few recent instances, the parent is not registered, while one or more of the subsidiaries is.

The regulator has criteria that it takes into account before approving new group structure arrangements. These include demonstrating the benefits to residents and improving the organisation's financial strength. It has set out detailed guidance to protect publicly-funded investment and prevent unplanned leakages of public funds into private ventures. It expects the parent or holding organisation to stand behind and support subsidiaries that are publicly funded, but not allow public funds to support subsidiaries that are funded in other ways.

Advantages and drawbacks

The main reasons for establishing groups are:

- to facilitate mergers that preserve the identity of the organisations that are coming together;

- to facilitate stock transfers from local authorities by promoting local identity and local accountability;

- to create appropriate governance oversight for each main business stream;

- to ensure that both charitable and non-charitable activities can be undertaken.

The main drawback is that groups make governance arrangements more complex and expensive to administer. The parent's board has a responsibility both for its own organisation and for the whole group. The same is likely to be true of the chief executive and other senior staff.

For organisations that have subsidiaries, the important judgements are between flexibility and complexity. Many activities previously thought to be non-charitable are now thought to be possible for charities to undertake (at least under certain circumstances). As a result some of the original incentive for group structures has been removed, and several housing groups have chosen to simplify their structures and amalgamate parent and subsidiary companies. But the imperatives of achieving local identity and accountability may make group structures attractive to some larger organisations operating in several areas.

Governance in a group structure

Where various organisations form a group structure it is particularly important to be clear about the relationships between the different boards and committees.

Groups will always be led by a 'parent'. The board of the parent (often called the group board) will not only be responsible for its own affairs, it will also have overall responsibility for the affairs of its subsidiaries.

The role of the group board will always include setting the strategy and direction of the group as a whole, monitoring the performance of all group members and ensuring that all members remain financially viable and conduct their affairs properly. It will also need to make clear arrangements for reporting by the subsidiary boards and make the time to consider their reports.

The boards of subsidiaries will have the normal range of board responsibilities but will operate within the wider strategy for the group that is determined by the holding organisation's board.

If the group parent also manages housing directly or provides services to other group members, then the oversight of these activities will also form part of the group board's role.

Committees of the parent need to be clear whether their remit extends to subsidiaries (and, if so, how they report to the subsidiaries). There should be a framework of agreements between the member organisations of a group so that inter-group relationships are clear.

Arrangements within groups are usually regulated by agreements. These are commonly of two different types (but may in some instances be combined together). The first type of agreement sets out the understanding of the members of the group about the role, powers and responsibilities of the parent. In groups that allow subsidiaries a fair amount of autonomy, this is sometimes referred to as a 'step-in' agreement as it includes the circumstances in which the parent is entitled to take control of the subsidiary.

The second type of agreement sets out the services that may be provided between group members. Most commonly the parent will provide financial and other central services. But in some cases services are provided by other group members both to the parent and to each other. Such agreements are usually called service level agreements and they generally define the services, set the standards and agree how such issues as cost or service delivery problems will be resolved.

In all cases, the group board has a responsibility for ensuring that each subsidiary has:

● written terms of reference;

- clearly defined delegation and reporting arrangements;

- clear links to the group board.

Committee or subsidiary structures complicate the organisation's delegation framework and can absorb considerable servicing resources. Parent boards should ensure that the organisational structure is kept as simple as possible and that its value is worth the time and resources invested in it.

Finding out more

Groups, mergers and alliances, KPMG LLP. National Housing Federation, 2007.

B7 What is the job of the chair?
In brief

The two most important leadership roles within an organisation are the chair and the chief executive. The chair's job is to lead the board and ensure that it governs the organisation effectively and has a collaborative relationship with the executive. The chief executive leads the staff, implements strategy and manages the delivery of services.

In more detail

How chairs are chosen

Formally the chair is elected by the board at the first board meeting after each annual general meeting. Board members should have in mind the particular skills that the role requires when deciding who should carry it out.

Rather than selecting one of their number to fulfil the role, increasingly boards are seeking to recruit someone suitably qualified for the role, and viewing it as a post that is remunerated and advertised.

Leading the board

The chair's principal task is to lead the board and ensure that it makes an effective contribution to the governance of the organisation. This involves:

- ensuring the efficient conduct of the business at board meetings and at general meetings;

- ensuring that the organisation provides appropriate role profiles and competency frameworks for all board members;

- building a constructive relationship with and between other board members;

- ensuring that all board members have an opportunity to express their views;

- ensuring that appropriate standards of conduct and behaviour are maintained in accordance with an agreed code of conduct;

- establishing a constructive working relationship with, and providing support for, the chief executive and ensuring that the board as a whole acts in partnership with the executive;

- taking responsibility for managing the performance of the chief executive against set objectives (appraisal is sometimes conducted by the chair and sometimes by a delegated group of board members);

- ensuring that the board delegates sufficient authority to committees, the chair, the chief executive and others to enable the business of the organisation to be carried out effectively between meetings of the board; and also ensuring that the board monitors the use of these delegated powers;

- ensuring that the board receives professional advice when it is needed, either from senior staff or from external sources;

- ensuring that the organisation complies with the Federation's Code of governance;

- taking decisions delegated to the chair between meetings, with the advice of the chief executive (and reporting back to the board).

Chairing meetings

Effective chairing is an essential component for well conducted meetings. Boards and committees are notorious for spending too much time on small matters while they nod through the big ones. Meetings can be poorly structured, papers can be tabled without the chance for proper consideration, and too much time can be spent re-discussing old issues.

An over-dominant chair can push through business without proper debate and leave other members feeling marginalised. A weak chair can permit interminable meetings that do not get through the business and frequently result in unclear decisions. This can leave members feeling angry and frustrated. Or there may be individuals who deflect attention from key issues and make meetings ineffective for their peers.

Boards are well advised to choose a chair with the necessary skills and experience. But part of the responsibility lies with all board members to exercise self-discipline and give support to a chair who is coping with trying circumstances. If meetings are not as productive as you feel they should be, raise this with colleagues to see if they share your views. If they do, then raise the matter with the chair or at one of the regular board effectiveness discussions.

Leading board appraisal

Regular appraisal, both of the performance of the board as a whole and of the performance of individual members, helps to maintain effectiveness. Part of the chair's remit is to take a lead in board appraisal. From time to time the board also needs to review its composition, the skills and experience of its members, and ensure that action is taken to remedy any deficiencies. Both these tasks may be delegated to a committee or group of members.

Being appraised

It is good practice for the chair to undergo appraisal, often on a 360 degree basis, with all board members and senior staff having the opportunity to comment confidentially to an objective third party on the chair's performance. Where a chair is not performing well, appraisal is the key to moving forward. This will preferably involve offering support targeted at improving performance (for example, through coaching or mentoring), but if necessary by creating the conditions for the chair to be replaced.

Leading the relationship with the chief executive and staff

At the heart of the board/staff relationship is the relationship between the chair and chief executive. A partnership approach based on mutual respect for each other's roles is essential in securing a productive and professional working relationship. They must both be sensitive to the requirements of their different roles and not try to do the job of the other. Trust and confidence in both directions are essential. The chief executive should be proactive in talking through issues and problems. The chair should be available to listen, debate, support and counsel.

The chair will also take a lead in appraising the performance of the chief executive and determining the remuneration of the chief executive and other senior staff. When necessary, he or she will lead on ensuring that the chief executive is replaced in a timely and orderly fashion.

The ambassadorial role

The chair has an important ambassadorial role representing the organisation on occasion, both externally and internally to residents and staff. The extent and prominence of the role will be a matter for discussion and agreement by the board and the chief executive.

Finding out more

Lost in Translation: A complete guide to chair/chief executive partnerships. NCVO, 2006: www.ncvo.vol.org.uk.

Read through the chair's role description and person specification.

B8 What does the chief executive do?

In brief

The chief executive leads the executive and the staff team. His or her role is to provide leadership and drive the housing association's business forward while remaining fully accountable to the board; manage the affairs of the organisation; maintain financial viability and control; and ensure that the executive and staff work collaboratively with the board.

In more detail

The chief executive leads the staff team. His or her responsibilities will include:

- managing the affairs of the organisation in accordance with its vision, values and objectives and the general policies and specific decisions of the board;

- helping the board determine strategies and policies;

- ensuring that the board receives advice on matters concerned with its governing instrument (rules), the law and the requirement to remain solvent;

- drawing the board's attention to matters that it should consider and decide;

- ensuring that the board is given the information necessary to perform its duties;

- leading and managing the staff of the organisation and ensuring that their performance is appraised;

- ensuring that proper systems of control are established and maintained;

- supervising, with the guidance of the chair, the preparation of documents for the consideration of the board;

- helping the chair ensure that the business of the board is properly conducted;

- ensuring that relationships between the senior staff and the board are positive and focus on the business of the organisation; and

- representing the organisation on occasions.

The responsibilities of the chief executive will be set out in the job description and contract of employment, but will also be affected by other plans and policies. The contract of employment must meet legislative requirements and deal with such matters as:

- the general duties and performance expected;

- how performance is monitored and remuneration determined;

- how complaints and disciplinary matters will be dealt with; and

- the length of contract and/or notice period.

The chief executive as a board member

In some cases, the chief executive (and sometimes other executives as well) will also be a board member, whether co-opted or elected. This creates certain conflicts of interest which have to be managed, but can be a good way of creating a unified top leadership team.

Finding out more

Good Governance: The Chief Executive's Role. NCVO, 2007: www.ncvo-vol. org.uk.

The role of the managing director/chief executive – Factsheet. IoD: www.iod. com.

Read through the chief executive's role description and person specification.

B9 What do other board officers do?

In brief

Other board officers like the vice-chair, treasurer, committee chairs and portfolio holders fulfil particular roles on behalf of the board. However, when it comes to making decisions about the housing association, all board members must take them together.

In more detail

The key role of the company secretary

The company secretary has duties set out in company law to ensure compliance with the organisation's governing document and various legal matters. The main duties are to:

- give notice of, supervise preparation for, and attend board and general meetings;

- supervise the preparation of all statutory returns; and

- keep the association's seal and maintain statutory registers of shareholding membership, mortgages and charges, interests of board members and staff, and hospitality and gifts.

The company secretary may be a member of staff, not necessarily the chief executive. He or she is directly responsible to the board for the formal responsibilities held.

Vice chair

The vice chair supports and deputises for the chair and fulfils any of the duties if the chair is absent or unavailable. He or she may also have a specific role like taking an overview of board committees or informing the chair of any concerns that board members have about the conduct of the board. Some organisations do not find it necessary to have a vice chair, with committee chairs deputising when necessary.

Chair of the finance committee

The chair of the finance committee (sometimes called the treasurer, though this title is becoming less common) leads on finance matters. Typically, the chair's role is to:

- oversee and present budgets, accounts, management accounts and financial statements to the board after discussion with the finance director, where applicable;

- ensure that the association keeps proper accounts and records and that financial resources are spent and invested in line with the association's policies, good practice and legal and regulatory requirements;

- be instrumental in the development and implementation of financial, reserves and investment policies.

Committee chair

Committee chairs lead the board's work within the remit of the particular committee. In addition to leading the particular committee and chairing committee meetings, committee chairs also act as a link to the relevant lead executive team member.

The role of committees is primarily to advise the board or carry out work delegated to them by the board. It is unusual, however, for staff to be operationally accountable to a committee in any way. Often committee members feel most comfortable problem solving and directing action (the management's job). Committee chairs have to take particular care to ensure the committee sticks to its remit and develops a strong working partnership with the lead executive and other staff.

Champions and portfolio holders

Housing associations with more streamlined committee structures often find it useful for one or more board members to take a lead on particular aspects of its work. This can be helpful on cross-cutting themes, such as value for money, or equality and diversity. Board champions or portfolio holders provide a link between the board and particular executive staff. This strengthens the partnership approach and allows more detailed scrutiny and more in-depth strategic input into developing proposals, while avoiding the bureaucracy that standing committees entail. Boards need to guard, however, against assuming that having a portfolio holder has relinquished the whole board's responsibility for a particular area of work.

Finding out more

ICSA Model Role Description for a Charity Treasurer (England & Wales). ICSA, 2007.

If your board has champions or portfolio holders, read through what is expected of them in their roles.

B10 Are board members who are tenants different?
In brief

All board members have a legal duty to put the association's best interests ahead of all other interests. Tenants who are board members have the same responsibilities as any other board member and cannot be 'delegates' or 'representatives' of other tenants. Nor can their views be expected to be 'representative' or 'typical' of other tenants.

Tenants who are board members bring their particular perspectives, experience and expertise to the work of the board, in the same way as other board members do. While this can lead to difficulties on occasion, and uncertainties as to when there might be a conflict of interest, tenant board members make a key contribution to effective housing association governance.

In more detail

How tenants are elected/selected

Tenant board members are usually selected in one of five ways:

- nominated representative – nominated or elected by tenants through local or regional structures such as tenants associations or area committees. (Some organisations like the accountability link to other forms of tenant representation. For others, this route of selection unhelpfully encourages the nominated tenants to see themselves as spokespersons for these bodies rather than board members);

- direct election – elected at the annual general meeting by the shareholding membership of the association alongside other board members (shareholding membership is usually open to anyone who is interested in supporting the work of the association and many associations encourage tenants to become members, although sometimes an association's rules limit the number of tenant shareholders to not more than one-third of all shareholders);

- election at public meetings – elected by all tenants in an area;

- a mixture of selection and election – whether put forward by tenants in different ways and then interviewed by a nominations committee or interviewed by a nominations committee prior to being allowed to stand for election; or

- individual selection or co-option – by the housing association.

All housing associations should have boards that contain a balance of suitably skilled and experienced members who are able to direct and control the organisation. Associations also have to comply with their rules and with charity law if the association is charitable.

Support for tenant board members

Sometimes the role can pose difficulties for tenants who are used to working in representative structures, where the main task is to advocate about issues, not to work together to make decisions and implement agreed plans. Housing associations should help tenant board members to contribute fully by providing:

- a statement of what is expected of board members;

- information, briefings and training;

- careful planning of meetings;

- expenses to ensure that members are not out of pocket;

- a code of conduct; and

- ongoing personal support to help recognise the different roles that tenants play in different situations, and how to perform them responsibly and work through any conflicts of interest.

The relationship with tenant groups and organisations

Board members have a legal duty to put the association's interests ahead of all others. This is known as a board member's 'fiduciary duty', and potentially may clash at times with a tenant's role as a tenant representative. While it is important to understand and accept the implications of this duty, it should not be seen as a bar to standing. Many board members face similar conflicts of interest from time to time, and all associations should have clear arrangements for disclosing and dealing with them.

Some of the ways to avoid any confusion are to:

- adopt a selection process which makes it clear that tenants are put forward as individuals, not as representatives;

- emphasise that all board members act as individuals and bring their particular experience and expertise to the board table. No one has a constituency as such; and

- have tenant consultation arrangements that do not rely on tenant board members. The board should be ensuring that the organisation engages effectively with tenants as a whole to understand their full range of views, opinions and needs, and their satisfaction with services.

Finding out more

Ensure that you are clear about the process by which tenants are appointed to the board in your organisation.

Read your organisation's code of conduct.

B11 What if I'm representing another organisation?

In brief

All board members, regardless of how they are nominated or elected to the board, have an overriding duty to put the housing association's interests ahead of all other interests. Nominees of other organisations cannot act as representatives of the other organisation when undertaking their board role.

In more detail

The legal position

All board members have a fiduciary duty to put the association's interests ahead of all others, including nominees from local authorities or other partner organisations. Such board members can make a valuable contribution to the work of a housing association even though they have responsibilities to others that might sometimes bring them into conflict with the association. Many board members face similar conflicts of interest from time to time.

Local authority representatives

Most associations formed by local authority transfer will have local authority nominees, who may be elected councillors. Such board members need to be subject to all the normal expectations of board members, such as confidentiality, appraisal, induction and training. Both the housing association and the local authority should have clear arrangements for disclosing and dealing with conflicts of interest that may arise from time to time.

Community and church representatives

The fiduciary duty to put the housing association's interests ahead of all others applies equally to community and church representatives.

Finding out more

Excellence in standards of conduct: Code for members. National Housing Federation, 2010.

The Code of Conduct: Guide for members. The Standards Board for England, 2007.

B12 Can executives be board members?

In brief

Executives can be board members, normally providing that they are in a clear minority, do not hold a board officer position or chair a main committee, and are not entitled to vote on matters where they might be seen as having a personal interest.

In more detail

The legal/constitutional framework

Historically, the Housing Corporation did not permit executives to be board members. This has now changed, and is now permitted, normally provided that such executives are in a clear minority. Executive board membership is only possible where the organisation's own rules permit – this may not be the case for some registered charities.

The board should agree on those matters on which executives should not be entitled to vote (including the election of chair and anything to do with executive remuneration). Non-executive board members should be in the majority at board meetings. The board's standing orders must clearly specify where they are to be excluded from decision-making. The board should agree those matters on which executive staff board members will not vote, for example, the membership of the remuneration committee, and should agree what core board committees it would be inappropriate for executive board members to sit on, such as the nominations or audit committees.

The special role of executives

Some larger associations have co-opted the chief executive and sometimes the finance director. A very small number has gone beyond this, with up to five executive board members. This can help to develop a 'one team' rather than a 'them and us' approach to board/executive arrangements.

Chapter C

You as a board member

A board is a team. Like any other team, it will only be effective if it is pulling in the same direction and can resolve differences of opinion amicably. A board has a right to expect that all its members will support the organisation's objectives and policies once these have been agreed.

Your collective responsibilities as a board member are matched by a series of more personal responsibilities. These should be set out in writing and agreed with you at the start of your board membership.

All organisations providing community services with the benefit of substantial public funding are in the public eye. The key role of housing associations in meeting housing need, and the substantial level of public investment, makes it essential that all those concerned with them operate to the highest standards of probity and conduct. Nothing can undermine public and government support more quickly than misconduct, or the muddling of self interest with public interest. Board members must not only set and maintain appropriate standards for their own conduct; they must take reasonable steps to ensure that these apply throughout the organisation.

C1 What are my responsibilities?

In brief

Each board member shares the responsibility, along with other board members, for directing the affairs of the housing association and ensuring it is solvent, well-run, and delivering the outcomes for which it has been set up, and that it complies with all relevant legal and regulatory requirements. Each board member also has a personal responsibility to:

- always act in the housing association's best interests;

- uphold the housing association's purpose, objectives and policies;

- uphold the values of the organisation through high standards of conduct and behaviour and by complying with the organisation's code of conduct, rules, standing orders and financial regulations;

- contribute to, and share responsibility for, the board's decisions, including its duty to exercise reasonable care, skill and independent judgement;

- prepare for and attend meetings;

- participate in reviews of board performance and measures designed to develop the board's capacity and effectiveness;

- declare any relevant interests and avoid conflicts of interest;

- respect the confidentiality of information; and

- ensure your skills are kept up to date and that you participate in training sessions.

In more detail

The legal and constitutional position

All board members must comply with company law and with the requirements of the Tenant Services Authority as regulator. If the organisation is a charity, board members must comply with charity law too.

The board must also, at all times, operate within the housing association's rules (or trust deed or memorandum and articles of association as appropriate). Every board member should have a copy of the organisation's rules or constitution and should be aware of its main requirements. Guidance on the rules should always be available from the association's company secretary.

Trustees and company directors

Depending on the form of incorporation, board members may be called 'board member', 'director', 'committee member' or 'trustee'. Although there are many names for board member, their central responsibilities are the same in all cases.

Anyone who is an undischarged bankrupt or barred from being a company director cannot be a board member. The housing association may also have rules that bar tenants who are in dispute with them from standing for the board, for example, anyone facing court action for rent arrears or who is barred from housing association office premises for violence or abuse.

The duty of care

Board members must use reasonable skill and care in their work as board members, using their personal skills and experience as needed, to ensure that the organisation is well-run and efficient. They must also consider getting external professional advice on all matters where there may be a material risk to the organisation, or where the board may be in breach of its duties.

> ## Finding out more
>
> Read your organisation's board member role description and person specification.

C2 How do I deal with conflicts of interest?

In brief

Board members must promptly declare any actual or potential interest which might possibly affect or influence their approach to a matter under discussion. If the conflict is clear and substantial, the board member should offer to withdraw from the meeting and, if invited to remain, refrain from participating in the discussion or the decision.

Until recently, legislation governed the handling of conflicts of interest (Schedule 1 of the Housing Act 1996) but this has now been repealed.

In more detail

The legal and constitutional framework

Board members have a fiduciary duty to put the association's interests ahead of all others and to always act in its best interests. 'Fiduciary' means 'acting on behalf of another' and a fiduciary responsibility should create a relationship of trust and confidence. It requires board members to act prudently, avoid taking undue risks, and avoid any personal conflicts of interest. Board members must ensure that their private or personal interests do not influence their decisions and that they do not use their position to obtain personal gain of any sort, other than agreed remuneration and expenses for being a member. Among the interests which board members must declare are both financial and non-financial ones, including:

- employment, in particular the name and business of employer(s);

- company directorships, business partnerships, self-employment, and significant shareholdings (previously defined as over 2 per cent of shares in a quoted company or 10 per cent in a private company);

- positions of public responsibility;

- membership of other organisations which might have a bearing on the housing association's work;

- any financial interest which might relate to the housing association's work;

- any other financial or non-financial interests (such as through a family member, a friendship or membership of an association, society, trade union, or the Freemasons or similar) which could be perceived as potentially affecting judgement or give the impression that a board member could be acting for personal motives.

It is not sufficient to act properly. The boards of all housing associations must be seen to act properly. Any impropriety is damaging personally, to the individual organisation, and to the whole sector. It is particularly important to declare any interests that could be relevant to your organisation's work and to avoid any situation where you could be construed as deriving a personal benefit from your board role.

The National Housing Federation Code of conduct

The National Housing Federation's Code of conduct requires housing association board members to:

- act according to high ethical standards and ensure that conflicts of interest are properly dealt with;

- not benefit from their position beyond what is allowed by law and is in the interests of the organisation;

- identify and promptly declare any actual or potential conflicts of interest affecting them; and

- have clear guidelines for receipt of gifts or hospitality.

When to declare an interest

Board members should be meticulous about declaring potential dualities or conflicts of interest and seeing that these are recorded in the housing association's register of interests. The register of interests is designed to protect both the association and individual board members by demonstrating openness, transparency and that there is nothing to hide, and should be available for public inspection upon request, subject to considerations of individual privacy.

A conflict of interest arises in any circumstance where doubt can be cast on a board member's ability to act with complete objectivity about the housing association's activities and solely in the best interests of the association. A member who has an interest, however slight, in any matter about to be discussed or decided by the board must disclose this interest. It is the individual board member's responsibility to take this action; he or she must not wait for someone else to challenge them on it.

A good test is to ask yourself whether someone else, knowing the relevant facts, would reasonably think your personal interest is so significant that it is likely to prejudice your ability to act solely in the best interests of the housing association.

The board member must not attempt to influence any other member's view or vote, nor the actions of staff, regarding the matter itself by any form of communication prior to, during or after, the relevant meeting(s).

Where such a conflict is likely to recur on a frequent basis, the board member should offer to resign. Any board member involved in a significant dispute with the housing association will usually be suspended until the dispute is resolved.

Claiming expenses

Board members, including those who are not paid, should be able to claim reasonable travel and other expenses incurred during their role as board members. Reasonable expenses might also include costs such as baby-sitting, care for dependent relatives, and direct costs of IT and communications. Each organisation should have a policy and a procedure for claims to be made.

Finding out more

Excellence in standards of conduct: code for members. National Housing Federation, 2009.

Understand how interests are disclosed in your organisation, and the correct process for claiming expenses.

C3   Do I have any personal liability?
In brief

It depends on the circumstances and the housing association's governing document. Board members who behave sensibly and prudently need have few worries about personal liability, but it is important to understand the position.

In more detail

The legal framework

A shareholding member of a housing association registered as an industrial and provident society, or as a company limited by guarantee, will have the benefit of limited liability. The limit of liability will be the £1 share (occasionally £5, depending on the rules).

A board member's potential liability can be greater because he or she is, together with other board members, ultimately responsible for the acts and failure to act of their organisation. If such acts or omissions result in losses then the individual members can, in some circumstances, be personally liable. This possible consequence must be taken seriously but the risks should not be exaggerated.

What it means in practice

Personal liability can only arise if a board member or members:

- act dishonestly or criminally, in which case no insurance will protect them;

- allow the organisation to operate when it is insolvent (known as 'wrongful trading' or sometimes 'fraudulent trading'), in which case the personal liability arises if debts are incurred when the board knew or ought to have known that they could not or would not be met;

- fail to make sure that the rules of the organisation are observed, in which case expenditure might be unauthorised or *ultra vires*; or

● fail to act with an appropriate level of prudence in carrying out their responsibilities.

This list is only a brief and simplified outline.

How to minimise the risk

There are no known cases where an individual board member of a housing association or company has been made personally liable. A conscientious board member is not likely to confront the circumstances when the risk becomes imminent but should always be ready to seek independent professional advice. The board as a whole always has the right to obtain such advice whenever it wishes. Every housing association should also have procedures to enable an individual member or minority of members to obtain advice if there are genuine grounds for concern.

Insurance against such personal liability is provided by the Federation to all its members. As a first and essential step every board member should check that their organisation is covered by the Federation's policy and that all conditions have been complied with, such as disclosure of relevant facts. Additional cover can also be arranged.

Finding out more

Check that your organisation has insurance cover for your personal liability.

C4   How much of my time will it take?

In brief

This will depend entirely on the housing association's size and activities. Many board members of larger associations find that they need to give the equivalent of about a day a month.

In more detail

Board members

Being a board member will involve preparation for and attendance at board meetings, and often also at other meetings and events. It is essential that board members are able to devote enough time to the essential duties involved. Housing associations should be able to give an idea of the expected time commitment to potential board members as part of the recruitment process. As noted above, a day a month is not unusual, but in some cases, more may be expected for a complex organisation, or one with a range of committees.

The chair

Chairs need to be able to make a more substantial time commitment. For a large association this can be anything up to a day a week.

Committee chairs and office holders

The time commitment will vary – clearly, it will lie somewhere between the major time commitment expected from a chair and that expected of a board member.

Finding out more

To find out more, speak to the chair or company secretary of your organisation.

C5   What induction can I expect?

In brief

All new board members need information and help to enable them to get up to speed and participate fully as quickly as possible. This should include a statement of expectations and a job description, an information pack explaining how the organisation works, and induction to bring you up to speed about the organisation and its activities.

In more detail

The induction process

You should not just be thrown in at the deep end and expected to pick up what is going on by attending successive board meetings. You have a right to proper induction, and any well run organisation should be able to provide it. If induction is not offered, then demand it. Systematic induction should include an information pack (or governance manual), typically containing some or all of the following:

- the rules of the organisation;

- the terms of reference of the board and any committees, and a list of members;

- a statement of your role as a board member (for example, as set out in the Federation's Code of governance);

- a statement of the role of the chair;

- an index of the housing association's main policies;

- board appraisal criteria and process;

- the framework of delegation to staff, including the chief executive's job description;

- financial and other standing orders;

- a corporate/business plan setting out what your organisation is trying to achieve, together with financial forecasts and the latest management accounts;

- a copy of the most recent annual report and accounts;

- a brief history of the organisation;

- a list of addresses, telephone numbers and email addresses for the organisation (including any regional or area offices if appropriate);

- a diagram of the staff structure with names of senior staff;

- a diagram of the board and committee structure (if appropriate);

- a list of the names, addresses, telephone numbers and email addresses and brief description of all board and committee members;

- key regulatory guidance, such as the regulatory framework;

- a full set of the last board meeting papers; and

- a list or chart of forthcoming board and committee meetings.

Induction should also include the following:

- meeting with the chair and other senior board members;

- observing a board meeting;

- meeting with the chief executive and other senior managers;

- a tour of some of the organisation's homes (not just the best ones) and to meet tenants as well as see bricks and mortar.

Finding out more

Ask the chair or company secretary of your organisation to provide you with details of the induction programme and ensure that you have participated in a skills audit when you first join an association.

C6 How will my work be appraised?

In brief

From time to time boards should step back and consider their collective effectiveness, and also have a process for appraising the performance of individual board members. Individual appraisal often involves self-assessment and a confidential discussion with the chair. The emphasis should be on improving how the board operates, and be a positive opportunity to explore how individual members can perform even better, and identify any development needs that they may have.

In more detail

Why appraisal matters

The board plays a central role in the organisation. It is important that board members contribute as effectively as possible, both individually and collectively, and there is almost always scope to develop capabilities and improve effectiveness.

How appraisal works

Appraisal recognises the value and importance of the contribution that board members make to the work of the organisation. The board should establish arrangements to appraise the contribution of individual board members and the chair. This should be carried out after the first year in office and thereafter at not more than three-yearly intervals. The best systems invite feedback through a 360 degree process, ie, from colleagues above and below in the organisation, but also potentially from people outside the organisation.

Many board members are part-time volunteers and may be unused to having their contribution evaluated. It is important that the experience is positive and constructive and focuses on enabling members to perform even more effectively. An independent external adviser can increase confidence and help calm fears.

Getting ready to be appraised

All board members have a shared purpose in taking steps to ensure that the board works as effectively as possible.

No one is perfect and everyone has strengths and weaknesses. Most people are well aware of the value of their contributions, the particular strengths that they bring to the board and aspects of their performance that could be enhanced or improved. Self-reflection and self-evaluation in advance provide a good basis for a constructive discussion.

Getting ready to appraise

Appraisals should be framed with reference to the job specification and required standards of behaviour. The focus should be on appreciating contributions and identifying any development needs, and where necessary agreeing a plan for how these can be addressed. Any criticisms should be specific and include suggestions for how to do things better in future. The discussion should be confidential, with the outcome reported to the board.

Finding out more

Achieving excellence: Board appraisal, Ann Gibson. National Housing Federation, 2007.

Read through the appraisal methodology used by your organisation.

C7 What support will I get for learning?

In brief

All housing associations will want to ensure that board members are fully equipped to contribute to the best of their abilities and really add value to the work of the organisation. All board members should receive regular briefings and training events to keep them abreast of issues and developments, and to refresh and enhance their knowledge and skills.

In more detail

Personal development and learning

It is really important that the board members of all organisations keep up to date and in touch with the many changes in the external environment. A failure to do so will undermine the organisation's ability to achieve its objectives and may lead to a failure to comply with new legislative or regulatory requirements.

The easiest and most obvious source of briefing for board members is from staff and other board members. Board papers should include a summary of any major changes in the external environment, and might also include more local information relevant to your organisation's work.

Inside Housing published by Ocean Media Group is a weekly publication specifically for people with an interest in social housing. It has an extensive website where you can also subscribe to daily bulletins. A housing association of any significant size should be prepared to provide all of its board members with a directly mailed copy. In addition, there is a number of other social housing publications with more of an emphasis on feature articles. These include *Roof* (from Shelter) and *Social Housing*.

The National Housing Federation publishes a substantial number of guides and booklets on a wide range of topics. Several have been written specifically for board members. There are also many other useful booklets published by the Chartered Institute of Housing, the Joseph Rowntree Foundation, Shelter and others, as well as guidance on websites, such as that of Communities and Local Government. These sources are particularly useful if you have a specific interest that you would like to develop further.

In-house training

Your organisation should take the trouble to identify your specific training needs. It is likely that you have experience and skills in some areas but may feel less knowledgeable about others. These gaps can be filled systematically through training. Some of this may be organised by the association itself. Sometimes it may involve attending a specific training event for board members of various housing associations. Training with other board members of your organisation has the added benefit of helping to build good working relationships and a shared understanding.

External training

You should also be willing to attend training events, individually or with the board, to expand your knowledge and keep up-to-date.

External training or attendance at housing conferences (of which there are several each year) has the advantage of allowing you to swap experiences with board members of other housing associations.

Coaching and mentoring

Coaching and mentoring can be a very useful way to enhance performance by helping people think things through or plot a course through a tricky situation, or to flourish in an environment that they are unused to. Many chief executives have coaches or mentors, and increasingly chairs are doing so as well. Some larger organisations have been investing in coaching for tenant and other board members.

Conferences and events

The Federation runs a range of specialist conferences (including one for board members) as well as its main annual conference. All of them include a wide range of events with opportunities to pick and choose sessions and workshops that are of interest to you. It also runs regional conferences that will address more local issues. A wide range of other bodies run training events and conferences and it would be easy to spend more time at them than on your own organisation's business. Selectivity is an important factor.

Qualifications and courses

There is a small number of courses and qualifications specifically aimed at board members, and other more general courses that may be relevant.

Finding out more

Find out whether your organisation has a board learning and development plan, and what kind of support is more widely available to you.

C8   How should I behave in board meetings?

In brief

All board members share a responsibility for contributing to, and taking responsibility for, board decisions. All board members should come prepared by reading the papers beforehand, be courteous at all times, and work constructively with the chair and other members to arrive at the best possible decisions in relation to the matters under discussion.

In more detail

Preparing for meetings

However expert or experienced you may be, being a board member requires a commitment to prepare for meetings. Attendance is clearly important, but attending without reading the papers for the meeting is discourteous to those who have prepared them and to your board colleagues. It is also likely to make you an ineffective member.

Making a contribution

The board needs a wide range of skills and experience and will only function effectively if each member is contributing fully. Contributing is about using your skills, experience and time to help the board reach good decisions.

Board meetings mostly involve considering reports and proposals prepared by staff (and occasionally by other board members or the chair). Board members will want to be satisfied that proposals are robust and accord with their priorities, and that any poor performance is being properly identified and addressed. And if not, to ensure the board agrees a suitably changed or strengthened proposal or plan of action. Achieving this is likely to require a mix of seeking clarification or explanation about matters that are not clear, influencing other people's views and building consensus for a particular solution or priority.

Keep contributions brief and to the point. Listen carefully to what other people have to say. Appreciate and build on what others have said. Try to understand what lies behind what people are saying and any restrictions they may be under. If reasons or motivations aren't obvious, ask a 'why' question.

The board has to reach decisions on many issues and will normally seek a consensus. Board members share responsibility for all board decisions and cannot pick and choose those with which they would like to be associated. But if your board makes a major decision with which you fundamentally disagree, and you have made your point of view clearly, then you may need to consider your position as a board member.

Constructive challenge

The process of holding to account inevitably focuses the spotlight on detail and what's not working well. This risks losing sight of the bigger picture. People are generally keen to be helpful, and are more comfortable problem-solving and directing action than thinking about 'vision' and 'being strategic'. It is easy to get drawn into trying to tell staff what to do to sort things out.

'Vision' means keeping in mind 'where we want to get to' and 'strategic' means 'making a plan', or identifying and tackling the underlying issues, looking beyond the symptoms to find and put in place a cure. The challenge is to focus on what is important, defining the outcomes board members want to see and assessing how well the organisation is achieving the outcomes (and not get drawn into the procedures for achieving them – that's the staff's job).

Constructive challenge requires an atmosphere of mutual trust and a commitment to continuous improvement. Board members need to be able to support and criticise at the same time. The board/executive relationship should be neither too cosy nor overly critical.

Confrontation puts people on the defensive. Praise good performance. Ask questions and give opportunities for staff to explain performance. Appreciate frank admission of failure or poor performance. If it is necessary, criticise performance or behaviour, not the person. Use temperate language ('below average' or 'not as good as we would like' rather than 'appalling' or 'terrible'). Try to avoid putting staff on the spot. If you have a question, let them know beforehand to give them a chance to research an answer.

Setting an example

How board members behave sets the tone for the organisation. Always maintain a high standard of personal behaviour towards other board members and staff. Be courteous to everyone and appreciate and respect differences – in knowledge, background, ability to speak in public etc. Avoid intemperate, provocative, offensive or obscene language. Respect the confidentiality of sensitive personal or organisational information.

Finding out more

Excellence in standards of conduct: Code for members. National Housing Federation, 2009.

Read your organisation's code of conduct.

C9   What will I need to do between meetings?

In brief

In addition to attending board and committee meetings, board members also need to devote enough time to other essential duties like dealing with urgent matters, representing the organisation at events, keeping up to date with the external environment and spending time with staff and residents.

In more detail

Dealing with urgent matters

Occasionally, a decision may be required urgently between board meetings. The board should have an agreed procedure for dealing with urgent matters. Some organisations have rules which allow a unanimous written board resolution to be passed between meetings. In other cases, the chair may have delegated authority to make a decision by 'chair's action', either alone or in conjunction with a small board urgency committee. Depending on the issue, the chair may also seek other board members' views before approving a course of action.

Other duties

Some board members must be willing to take on additional roles, including chairing committees of the board, or sitting on appeals panels. Many boards have regular liaison meetings with residents. On major issues there may be a need to attend other meetings as part of the preparation for a board meeting. There will also be occasions when you need to represent the organisation at external events.

Staying up to date

Running a housing association can be complex and board members need to be up to date on the operating environment. This may involve wider networking, taking up training opportunities, or reading the relevant specialist trade magazines.

Spending time with staff and residents

It is also a good idea for board members to spend some time on the 'front line', with staff and tenants. This needs some planning and 'ground rules', to create opportunities that work well, and do not create false expectations on either side. Job shadowing can work well, as can programmes of visits to certain areas and projects. In exploring good practice, it is helpful too to visit other organisations. Board members need to avoid, however, seeing this kind of activity as encouragement to become overly operational.

Finding out more

Discuss with the company secretary or chair how you can help support the work of the board between meetings.

C10 Will I be paid?

In brief

It depends on the approach adopted by the housing association. In most smaller housing associations, board members are voluntary and unpaid, apart from being reimbursed for out of pocket expenses such as travel and child care.

As housing associations have become larger and more complex businesses, the time commitment expected of board members has risen substantially, and increasingly board members are paid. Rising expectations of board members contribute to rising governance standards.

In more detail

Why payment is used

All organisations are expected to strive for continual improvement in their governance (as in other areas of their work) irrespective of whether or not they choose to pay board members.

Housing associations are now operating in an increasingly complex, fast moving, risky environment, attempting to meet rising resident expectations against a backdrop of greater scrutiny, and increasing difficulty of developing new homes. These pressures are placing much greater demands on governance structures, requiring levels of commitment that go beyond what it is reasonable to ask of volunteers. Also board members and staff now regularly come into contact with other public sector organisations that pay board members (or allowances for councillors).

Payment is a way to:

- emphasise the importance of board members' governance responsibilities;

- formalise the expected commitment; and

- provide some recompense for the expected level of commitment.

Payment brings added requirements to be transparent about how payment levels are set, reviewed and published. It also makes open recruitment essential. But for the most part, all organisations will be seeking to meet the same high standards. Not paying cannot be an acceptable excuse for a lower standard of governance.

The legal framework

Until 2004, legislation prevented all but a handful of housing associations from paying their board members. Housing associations are now permitted to pay their board members. Where an organisation wishes to pay its board members, it should first satisfy itself that it has the power to do so under its constitution and, if not, seek approval for a rule change from the necessary authorities.

Schemes of payment

Both the Tenant Services Authority and the National Housing Federation are neutral about the issue of paying board members. Both have put out detailed guidance on the issues that should be taken into account before coming to a conclusion. The TSA expects that associations will – before paying – have prepared a 'business case' that sets out how payment will help to strengthen effective governance.

Setting payment levels

The guidance issued by the National Housing Federation includes suggested limits on payment levels for different sizes of association. Payment at these levels should cost less than 0.5 per cent of an organisation's turnover.

People on benefits

Payments may have implications for benefit entitlements, so it is essential that anyone in receipt of state benefits who is thinking of standing for a board should ask about any payments and seek advice about how their benefit entitlement might be affected by any such payments.

Finding out more

Board member pay: Principles and practicalities. National Housing Federation, 2009.

Trustee expenses and payments, CC11. Charity Commission, 2008.

You can also contact the National Housing Federation directly for latest details of trends in board member pay (check the Publications section of the website first).

Chapter D

Running the business

Housing associations have social objectives and clear values. While maintaining the financial strength to achieve objectives is clearly crucial, achieving a profit is not the primary objective (indeed associations must be not-for-profit organisations). Running an organisation with social objectives is harder – not easier – than running a business for profit. This is because a wider range of judgements is involved. Determining the right course of action when purely financial objectives conflict with social objectives is part of the challenge and satisfaction of being a housing association board member.

However, having social objectives is not just a matter of 'doing good' in some vague or unspecified way. If social objectives are going to drive the business effectively then it is crucial that they are well focused and clearly articulated. The fact that housing associations do not have the objective of distributing profits to shareholders does not justify being un-business-like. Unmet housing need is growing and it is incumbent on all housing associations to make the greatest contribution that they can within the resources available to them. Their resources are also directly derived from rents paid by tenants, many of whom will be on very low incomes. This means not wasting resources and being as efficient and economical as possible. Many business techniques are therefore very relevant, even though they are being applied to meet social rather than profit objectives.

The success of any board depends heavily on its ability to handle general management and financial issues. Success in specialist areas will rarely compensate for general management or financial weaknesses. The board has a particular role and responsibility for maintaining an overview of the organisation's work and making sure that its different activities combine into an effective and viable whole.

D1 How do we set the mission?

In brief

A clear organisational mission or purpose which acts as a focus for everything the organisation does is a hallmark of good governance.

Every housing association has its own purpose and mission. The mission should take account of the views and priorities of all the principal stakeholders (people and organisations with a legitimate interest in, or who provide resources for, the work of the housing association). This is likely to include tenants and other beneficiaries, potential beneficiaries, local communities, local authorities, funders, regulators and the government.

In more detail

The key role of the board

The board determines the focus of a housing association's work and is the main custodian of the organisation's core purpose and core values. The path of a housing association is likely to be strewn with constraints, threats and temptations. Tailoring the organisation's work to maximise grant funding (following the money) or following the line of least resistance in other areas can make life easier in some respects but may deflect the organisation from its core objectives.

As external circumstances change, the fundamental objectives to achieve the mission may need to be reviewed and redefined. Tempting opportunities may arise to develop new areas of work. Funding arrangements may change, making a previous area of work impossible. The organisation's objectives must be reconciled with what is practicable and achievable without compromising its core purposes.

Boards must also be mindful of the long-term consequences and the wider impact of their decisions, for example, in relation to environmental concerns and how existing and future homes are maintained and rendered more energy efficient.

These are weighty matters that deserve proper board consideration. Finding time for strategic thinking can be an uphill struggle in the context of crowded board agendas with many items for decision.

The golden thread

A clear statement of the organisation's purpose and mission should guide the setting of all strategies, objectives and plans, and guide employee's actions and decisions at all levels of the organisation. Every staff member should be able to see how their job contributes to achieving the organisation's mission.

Finding out more

Read your organisation's plans, annual reports – focus on the mission statement and the values set out.

D2 What do I need to know about finance?

In brief

The board has overall responsibility for the financial health and viability of the organisation and must make sure that effective financial control arrangements are in place. Key elements are:

- business plans and budgets that outline the organisation's resource requirements;

- management accounts and cash flows to monitor performance through the year;

- effective financial controls and procedures; and

- treasury management for associations with substantial borrowings or cash resources.

In more detail

The key drivers

Financial management is an essential element of good corporate governance and forms the basis of accountability to stakeholders for the stewardship and effective use of resources.

In legal terms, board members are the equivalent of directors of a company and must take prudent steps to ensure that the organisation can meet its commitments. Having social objectives is no excuse for being careless or imprudent with financial resources. Maintaining financial control has a number of key elements. First, the board must be clear that it has the resources for its planned operations. The business plan and annual budget are particularly important in this respect. The board may find it helpful to delegate detailed scrutiny of both to a finance committee. If it does so, it should be clear that it is not diluting the board's overall responsibility.

Second, the board must also be satisfied that there are effective arrangements for managing the budget. This will require a hierarchy of management oversight of all areas of the budget (both income and expenditure) and individual responsibility for the controllable elements (usually called budget holding).

While business plans and cash flows will enable the board to see that planned resources should be sufficient to meet planned commitments, plans frequently go awry. Knowing what has actually happened is equally important and provides a pointer to the reliability of the plans themselves. While there may be separate measures of key items (such as rent arrears), it is only management accounts and reports against the budget that provide a full picture. Quarterly management accounts and reports against the budget are an essential protection for the board, without which it cannot be satisfied that it is in control. The appropriate level of detail will depend on the size and complexity of the organisation's affairs.

Borrowing and investment

Housing associations need private finance to fund the cost of building new homes and undertaking major improvements to existing housing. Stock transfer associations also need private finance to fund the original purchase as well as the improvement programme.

Borrowing cannot be kept separate from the other activities. The starting point for raising private finance is a clear understanding of the organisation's overall financial situation, and how the future funding requirements for development and improvement sit within the context of the rest of the organisation's work. It is not sufficient to know this on a year-by-year basis. Housing associations are long-term, capital-intensive businesses with uneven patterns of expenditure. Some have a relatively new housing stock that is consequently less expensive to maintain. A positive cash flow at the present time might become a negative cash flow in the future when the organisation has to use its reserves to carry out major repair and refurbishment programmes.

Housing associations commonly borrow for longer than 25 years and must be satisfied that they are entering into commitments that they can meet throughout this time. These commitments are not just to make the payments required under the loan agreement. They also include undertakings (often referred to as covenants) to keep various financial ratios (such as the ratio of income to expenditure) in a healthy state and to maintain sufficient security for the loan. A breach of these covenants is as much a breach of the loan as non-payment and the consequences can be just as severe. It is therefore vital that the organisation has long-term financial projections that demonstrate that it can continue to meet its commitments.

Borrowing strategy

All housing associations have choices that they can make about the terms on which they borrow. The objective of an association's borrowing strategy is to borrow in a way that plays to the organisation's strengths and protects it against the uncertainties of economic forecasting. Central to the strategy will be the concept of achieving a balance of different types of loans. Unless the organisation has a high level of treasury management skills available to it, it should seek independent advice on these matters. In relation to loan terms, it should always take the advice of a suitably experienced solicitor.

Timing: borrowing early may mean that the organisation incurs unnecessary borrowing costs. Borrowing late leaves it vulnerable to last minute changes of mind by the lender and a cash flow crisis. Lenders are put off by last minute borrowing as it casts doubt on the organisation's management skills. Striking the right balance is a key strategic decision. It is possible to negotiate loans (called 'facilities') where the money is kept available by the lender but not actually borrowed until the housing association needs it. A prudent board will ensure that the organisation has the resources to meet its commitments over the next 12 months from existing facilities or its own resources.

Fixed and variable interest rates: most types of loans are available on either a fixed interest or a variable rate basis. If an organisation borrows on a variable rate basis then it is vulnerable to periods of high inflation as interest rates can rise steeply. If an organisation borrows on a fixed rate basis then it can be vulnerable to periods of low inflation when interest rates tend to fall. Taking decisions about fixed and variable interest rates is complicated because they do not always move up and down together or in line with inflation. If financial markets expect interest rates to fall, long-term rates may be lower than short-term rates and vice versa.

Using financial instruments: it is possible to insure against major fluctuations in interest rates, but this is often quite expensive and the financial instruments involved carry risks of their own. Most organisations will attempt to balance the risks by having a mix of fixed and variable rate loans. It is possible to borrow on the basis that loan payments are low to start with but increase over time. It is also possible to limit the extent of interest rate increases and decreases in variable rate loans. It is particularly important to seek advice with these more unusual forms of borrowing.

Loan terms: loans are available on widely different terms from different lenders. The cheapest (in terms of the lowest interest rate) may not be the best in other areas. Particularly important will be the lender's requirements for security and for key financial ratios. If your organisation has concerns about running out of security then it may be more advantageous to borrow from a lender with lower security requirements, even though it might be slightly more expensive. In terms of the requirement to maintain healthy financial ratios (commonly income : expenditure, rental income : loan repayments etc.), these are cumulative undertakings. Once you have agreed to provide them for one lender then you are stuck with them for the duration of that loan. Care should be taken not to enter into terms that are more onerous than those in your existing loans unless this is really necessary. It is essential to keep an accessible record of loan requirements so that the organisation is aware of its continuing obligations long after those who negotiated the loans have left.

Group-wide borrowing: a number of groups are now organising their borrowing on a group-wide basis so as to take advantage of the scale and flexibility that this can bring. There are different approaches and the appropriate route is likely to depend on the relative financial strength of group members as well as other factors. Some groups have established group borrowing vehicles.

Treasury management

A key element of financial control is to ensure that the organisation has the cash to meet all its commitments. There should be a detailed rolling annual cash flow as well as a medium-term cash flow matching the period of the business plan. However, cash forecasting is only the start.

Housing associations are typically cash-rich businesses with secure, rent-based cash flows. However, developing housing associations are also cash-hungry, as cash is required for their building or improvement programmes. They therefore need to borrow. Housing associations also need to put money aside for future repairs and to meet lump sum loan repayments. The task of managing these elements together is generally referred to as treasury management. The board must ensure that it has effective treasury management arrangements in place. These will include:

- short-term, medium-term and long-term cash flow projections;

- an appropriate borrowing strategy;

- effective arrangements for the investment of surplus cash;

- adequate borrowings to meet its forward commitments; and

- sufficient reserves of accessible cash to cope with unforeseen events.

Finding out more

Understanding financial statements: An overview of accounts for social housing providers, Desmond Gray. National Housing Federation, 2011.

Housing Association Finance. A comprehensive online guide produced jointly by the National Housing Federation and CIPFA; available at www.tisonline.net/housingfinance/default.asp.

Spend some time with the finance director to get briefed on key financial issues.

Consider going on a course or having some bespoke training for members of the board on understanding housing association accounts and finance and the board's role in this area.

D3   How should the board plan and budget?

In brief

Housing associations are long-term investment businesses as well as service providers. Boards need to be sufficiently forward-looking to plan for long-term commitments as well as agreeing clear short-term objectives, budgets and performance measures.

In more detail

Business planning

The wider objectives of the housing association are only likely to be achieved if they are translated into clear plans and strategies. Developing and updating a corporate and business plan on an annual basis is an essential management tool for any housing association large enough to employ staff. It helps to establish clear objectives for staff and helps to turn good intentions into reality. As important as setting clear objectives is the need to plan for and secure the necessary financial resources and maintain financial viability.

No one document can encompass such a range of tasks. Most housing associations (particularly those that are large and medium-sized) will find it helpful to distinguish between:

- mission statement and long-term objectives;

- long-term financial projections (at least 10 years and probably 25);

- medium-term business/corporate plan (rolling 3-5 years);

- annual operational plan; and

- annual budget and cash flow.

Approving strategies, plans, budgets and other statements of objectives is a core responsibility of the board. Developing them jointly with senior staff is essential to a healthy board/staff relationship. In practical terms, the bulk of the work will be undertaken by staff, but this does not mean that the board's role is limited to ratifying the result. The process must involve both board members and staff and exemplify the board/staff partnership.

Corporate and business plans are the medium through which the board sets the direction of the organisation and monitors performance. To be effective at a working level, plans need to contain:

- clear targets;

- clear measures of performance;

- clear timescales; and

- clearly assigned responsibility.

The annual cycle

An effective corporate and business planning process is likely to incorporate the following features:

- conducted on an annual cycle which provides time to move from the general to the particular;

- grounded in a reappraisal of the changing operating environment and the opportunities and threats that exist;

- informed by briefing papers for the board which identify strategic options and choices about priorities as well as their resource implications;

- involves staff at all levels as well as board members, so as to maximise commitment to the result;

- leads to general draft plans before they are worked up in greater detail; and

- results in detailed documents that are consistent with the board's directions, fully understood at all levels, and facilitate performance monitoring.

Long-term financial projections

Housing associations are long-term, capital-intensive businesses. Developing housing associations will frequently be borrowing over 20-30 year periods. They may borrow on a basis that involves repayment throughout the term of the loan or by a single payment at the end. They may borrow for shorter periods and rely on subsequent borrowing to repay the earlier loans. All of the borrowing will need to be secured and, at low grant rates, the organisation may need to offer security beyond the asset that it is purchasing. Organisations will also need to make sure that they have set aside (or can borrow and repay) the resources to maintain and refurbish an ageing stock.

An organisation can only make sound judgements about all these matters and whether it can sustain a particular development policy or rent policy if it makes long-term financial projections. These should be in sufficient detail to establish that the organisation will be able to meet its long-term commitments. For these purposes, 10-15 year projections may be sufficient. For housing associations with an uneven pattern of development and borrowing (such as large scale voluntary transfers) or with long-term stock reinvestment needs, the projections will need to match the term of their main loans. Investment partner associations are expected to provide 25-year financial projections.

All long-term projections have to make assumptions about what is going to happen to key variables that have an impact on income and expenditure. These key variables will include:

- inflation;

- interest rates;

- rent increases; and

- property values (important as security for loans).

No one knows what will actually happen in the future but this does not mean that it is not worth trying. In fact, it is very important for the board to have a clear sense of how changes in these key variables could affect the organisation's long-term health. It is also vital for the organisation to know whether it is following a course of action that can be sustained indefinitely, or whether it is likely to lead to financial difficulties.

Finding out more

Get hold of and read the budgets, and the reports. If they're not clear, ask the finance director or one of the finance team to sit down and explain the format to you, and go through the key issues.

D4   How much responsibility can the board delegate?

In brief

In all but the smallest organisations, the board's job is to decide strategic aims and to delegate sufficient authority and freedom to enable the chief executive and other senior managers to manage operational implementation effectively and meet the aims set by the board. But the board always retains ultimate responsibility for running the organisation.

The board sets the parameters within which the chief executive works on behalf of the board. It is important that board members do not concern themselves with levels of detail that are inappropriate for their role, while ensuring that they are not too far removed to provide effective oversight and scrutiny.

In more detail

The delegation framework

Housing associations come in all shapes and sizes. The size and complexity of the organisation's operations will have an impact on the board's role and therefore on the role of individual board members. As an organisation grows and employs more managerial staff, the board will find that its role needs to change. The larger the organisation the more the board has to delegate.

The scope of the delegation framework is likely to include:

- committee remits, membership and reporting arrangements;

- senior manager job descriptions, and staffing and line management structure;

- financial regulations, standing orders, limits of authority etc;

- policies and procedures;

- corporate and business plans and budgets;

- key decisions reserved for the board; and

- arrangements for monitoring and reviewing the delegation framework.

Clarity of delegation is an essential safeguard for the board and helps to achieve a clear and effective relationship with staff. It is important to ensure that it is well understood and implemented.

For larger organisations where there is substantial delegation, it is usually helpful to clarify what is not being delegated. A list of the matters that are reserved to the board helps to achieve clarity and provide reassurance that it controls the big decisions. For example:

- expansion into new activities or geographical areas;

- stopping a material part of the housing association's service or work;

- changes to the corporate structure;

- changes to the governance arrangements;

- approval of arrangements for and membership of any committees;

- appointment and removal of any board member or officer; and

- approval of key policies and the corporate plan.

Delegation to committees

Committees are able to go into issues in greater depth than is possible in board meetings and can provide opportunities for detailed scrutiny of performance and other matters. Committees generally work best if they have clear delegated authority to decide matters and report back on an exceptions basis in relation to their performance monitoring responsibilities. The board has a responsibility for ensuring that each committee has:

- written terms of reference;

- clearly defined delegations that do not cut across other delegations (for instance to staff); and

- clear links and reporting arrangements to the board.

Delegation to staff

At the heart of the way the board exercises control is the scope of its delegation to staff. This is defined in a number of different ways including:

- senior manager job descriptions;

- financial regulations, standing orders, limits of authority etc;

- policies and procedures; and

- corporate and business plans.

Job descriptions: the key job description for the board is that of the chief executive. It should cover the functions specified in B8. The board should also approve the job descriptions of the other senior managers.

Statements of delegation (who can do what) prescribe how matters are handled at different levels within the organisation. All housing associations will have financial regulations and standing orders. Larger organisations will find it helpful to set out a full range of what is delegated and to whom.

Policies and procedures (standards and how they are to be implemented) will be influenced by legislation, good practice guidance and outside parties such as the Homes and Communities Agency, other funders, and local authorities. Generally, it will be for staff to develop the details of policies and procedures, and for the board to approve and review them. Nevertheless, it is for the board to determine how they should apply in the organisation. While policies and procedures will often be detailed, their value and importance cannot be overstated. They help to ensure fair treatment and the quality and consistency of services. They also help to manage risk. The degree of detail can present boards with a dilemma. A focus on key aspects will avoid information overload.

Corporate and business plans (what we are trying to achieve) play a key role in defining the scope of delegation to the chief executive and other staff. The corporate plan sets out objectives and priorities and makes it easier to delegate implementation. It also makes it easier to define those issues that need to come to the board for a specific decision (for example, matters that do not accord with the corporate plan).

Financial delegations

All housing associations will have financial regulations and standing orders. These will cover such matters as the authorisation of expenditure, signing cheques and other documents, opening bank accounts and so on. Because the handling of money is so crucial, they are often dominated by financial issues. It is equally important that other types of transaction are covered. For larger organisations this might include the acquisition of schemes, building contracts, letting of homes, arrears action and employing consultants.

The business plan and more detailed annual budget establish the framework for budget holding. Expenditure within agreed budget heads can be delegated and the scope for varying budgets within the same total of expenditure (virement) can be agreed.

Monitoring delegations

In a tough and competitive environment, housing associations will face problems and opportunities that cannot be foreseen. There will also be other decisions of such importance that they should only be taken by the board. If the board tries to take too many decisions then it is likely to neglect other key aspects of its role. However, if it is taking very few, then it may be an indication that the organisation is underachieving or the board is not in effective control. As with so many aspects of the board's role, achieving the right balance of delegation and involvement is crucial.

Periodically, the various elements of the delegation framework will need to be reviewed and updated to ensure that they keep pace with changes in the organisation's circumstances.

Finding out more

Ask your company secretary to give you a copy of the delegations framework, and to explain anything that may not be clear. Find out how often the framework is revised, and what reports are made back to the board about use of delegated powers.

D5   How should the board manage risk?

In brief

Almost anything that helps an association to achieve its objectives will involve risk. Effectively managing risk involves developing a practical plan to identify and assess risks, agree appropriate responses and provide assurance that the chosen responses are effective; then regularly reviewing and updating the plan (or risk map) to take account of changing circumstances. The aim is to minimise the chance of unexpected events having a significantly adverse impact on the organisation.

In more detail

What risk means

A risk is the likelihood that a hazard will cause a specified harm to someone or something. Those involved in assessing risk usually have to balance the probability of harm occurring and the impact of that harm.

Managing risk is important when assessing new types of business but it is no less important when balancing conflicting priorities or facing changes in the external operating environment. Boards have to take many decisions involving risk. These might include:

- undertaking a major development;

- raising private finance;

- embarking on a new venture; or

- entering into a major contract to provide services.

Such major decisions can give a misleading impression about what risk management requires. Almost all activities can go wrong. Poor maintenance could result in an injury to a tenant or mean a much more expensive repair at a later date. Sloppy procedures could encourage a fraud. Under-insurance could lead to significant loss. A development opportunity might be missed because there is no cash reserve. Vulnerable residents could be mistreated by staff.

External events can have a serious impact. A contractor might go out of business. Extreme weather events may cause flooding or delay building programmes. Finance markets may become volatile or unpredictable and make it difficult or impossible to raise loan finance. Increasing energy prices or changes in welfare support may make it more difficult for vulnerable tenants to pay their rent.

The best way to manage risk is to ensure that all of the organisation's work is planned and managed effectively, and consideration of risk is an integral part of the management culture. At an operational level, organisations need to make sure that decision makers take risk into account as decisions are made. It is also important not to see risk just in financial terms. Associations rely heavily on their reputation and this can be damaged much more easily than it can be built up.

Risk mapping

The board will need to be clear about the organisation's ability to absorb risk and the extent to which it is willing to expose its resources. The first step is to build up a clear picture of the obstacles, weaknesses and threats that the organisation faces, and then prioritise them both in terms of their likelihood and potential impact. This is usually referred to as a risk map. The next step is to plan how to manage the identified risks to mitigate the potential impact. Responses will include implementing internal controls, insuring against the risk, terminating the activity that is causing the risk, modifying the risk or, in some circumstances, accepting the risk.

The role of committees

The board or committee's role is to oversee the risk management system and to take decisions on matters that involve significant risk for the organisation. What these are will depend on the size and focus of each housing association. For a small organisation that is not developing any new housing it may be a decision to undertake a major repair. For a medium-sized organisation it may be a decision to undertake a substantial development project. For a special needs agency it may be a decision to enter into a major care contract. For a large association or housing company it may be a decision to undertake a large development or repair programme without the benefit of external subsidy.

A board that tries to take too many decisions will have no time to give each one proper attention and will discourage staff from taking responsibility. The board should concentrate on those involving most risk and delegate the remainder. It should also be clear that taking the decision to proceed or not to proceed does not, of itself, manage the risk. Far more important is the quality of the preparatory work. There should always be an analysis of the possible risks and the steps that have been taken to minimise them, and the steps that would have to be taken if things go wrong. The board should be able to probe in order to satisfy itself that the detailed investigation has been thorough. It can then take an informed decision.

The toughest risk management decisions for a board will generally be those concerned with new ventures. It is nearly always riskier to do something for the first time as there is no previous experience to learn from. Risk appraisal procedures developed for other aspects of the organisation's work may not be entirely appropriate. Particular care should be taken with the financial and other projections. New ventures can also involve wider strategic issues (is this consistent with our objectives?) as well as complex financial judgements. They may also involve some discussion with the regulator, which takes a keen interest in diversification activities. It can be helpful to take external advice from people who have experience of such ventures elsewhere. Learning from other people's mistakes is one of the most economical ways of managing risks.

Finding out more

With the best of intentions: Learning from problem cases 3. Housing Corporation, 2007.

Make sure that your board has a risk map that is regularly reviewed.

D6   How can the board ensure things are done properly?

In brief

Boards usually use a mix of systems to enable them to be sure that the organisation complies with the law and regulatory requirements (compliance), carries out activities as intended and at required standards (internal controls), and checks that processes are operating effectively (assurance).

In more detail

Compliance

The board has overall responsibility for ensuring that the organisation complies with the requirements of all legislation that affects its work. It will generally be well advised to place a formal duty on the chief executive to advise it on these requirements and ensure that they are met. It should also recognise those situations where specialist legal advice to the board becomes appropriate.

Controls

'Internal control' covers all the arrangements that a housing association makes to ensure that it performs as it should. Effective internal control enables the board to be sure that its strategies, plans and delegation framework are being implemented properly throughout the organisation. As with risk management, effective internal control requires a total approach. The responsibility does not end with the appointment of an internal auditor or the establishment of an audit committee. Internal control requires attention to detail and compliance with appropriate policies and procedures at all levels. It is therefore primarily dependent on effective management at all levels. The board needs to be satisfied that the overall framework of control is in good shape and regularly reviewed. Internal and external audit then become the second line of defence, rather than the first.

Awareness of techniques for reinforcing internal control can help the board develop an effective framework, rather than having to rely on vigilance and the demotivating assumption that people are always trying to evade control. Such techniques include:

- separation of duties (so that more than one person has to be involved in important decisions);

- checklists and signing-off (so that staff have to initial that specific checks or procedures have been followed);

- restricting authority with the help of third parties (bank mandates or standing instructions to solicitors are common examples);

- effective training and induction (so people understand what is expected of them);

- internal agreements between departments (so that the quality and timeliness of internal services are specified); and

- openness of performance information (the more people know, the harder it is to hide mistakes).

Assurance

Although internal audit is often thought of as financial checking, this is to misunderstand its scope. Internal audit covers all the arrangements that an organisation makes to ensure that all its control systems are operating effectively and that staff (and others) are complying with policies and procedures. Managers and supervisory staff will be doing this as part of their normal responsibilities.

Internal audit is a more systematic way of checking that normal managerial processes are working effectively. It will involve a periodic review of all the organisation's control systems. It will test that procedures and policies are being followed and may also include special studies to test value for money. All of these matters will be reported to the board so that appropriate action can be taken. The independence of internal audit arrangements is a particular safeguard for the board.

The annual process

Management of internal audit by the board involves approving the internal audit programme, striking a balance between checking compliance, reviewing control systems, value for money studies, reporting and considering appropriate remedial action. It involves an assessment of the current priorities and of the resources that should be provided.

At least annually, the full board should receive a formal report from the audit committee (or equivalent body). This should cover:

- the adequacy of internal controls;

- the effectiveness of internal audit arrangements;

- the effectiveness of external audit arrangements; and

- compliance with internal controls assurance.

> **Finding out more**
>
> *Audit Committees: Combined Code Guidance* (the Smith Report). FRC, 2003: www.frc.gov.uk.
>
> *Review of the role and effectiveness of non-executive directors* (the Higgs Review). DTI, 2003: www.bis.gov.uk.
>
> *A wider role for internal audit,* Jane Bloodworth. National Housing Federation, 2004.

D7   How should the board manage performance?
In brief

Having set clear strategies and plans and a clear framework of delegation, the board must check that objectives are being achieved and the work of the organisation is progressing as intended. Managing performance effectively requires:

- a good reporting system that provides the information necessary to assess performance, usually a balance of:

  - performance information (outcome data, quantity and cost data, surveys, explanation of what the information means, benchmarking comparisons etc.), and

  - audit and inspection (a more in-depth look and a check on the accuracy of the information the board is receiving);

- regular review and corrective action if objectives are not being achieved (scrutiny and holding managers to account for performance).

In more detail
Performance monitoring and continuous improvement

Effective performance monitoring should be built around a clear sense of what should be happening. The intended course of action will be agreed in corporate and business plans and in the annual budget, cash flows and other operational plans. These provide a good basis for checking whether what is actually happening matches what should be happening, and are therefore of particular value to board members. If monitoring of these core documents shows that the organisation is broadly on target with all of them then it is unlikely that anything is going seriously wrong. These are the key areas, and no amount of special interest in other issues should deflect the board from monitoring them.

Attempting to monitor all aspects of what is going on is a certain recipe for drowning in detail. The key to successful performance monitoring by the board is to:

- concentrate on the key areas;

- use performance indicators (measuring outcomes where possible);

- insist on clarity of data and narrative explanations that pick out what is happening (both good and bad);

- use graphs that show performance trends in relation to targets rather than masses of data;

- be satisfied that the association's management information system delivers timely and accurate information to managers so that they can monitor and manage the detailed operations.

Performance monitoring should be going on at all levels within the organisation. It is best if the board concentrates on overall performance and on making sure that managers have the information they require to monitor and manage the detailed operations.

Scrutiny and holding to account involve working collaboratively with the chief executive and other senior staff continually to improve performance. The challenge is to focus on the outcomes the board wishes to see, and on assessing how well the organisation is achieving the outcomes and identifying and tackling any underlying issues that may be preventing the organisation from doing so. Avoid getting drawn into attempting to manage the service (that's the executive's job) or seeking someone to blame. In the majority of cases, poor performance ought to lead on to identifying a need for process review, or for support and training, or for increased resources.

Benchmarking with others

All performance is relative. Benchmarking provides a way of assessing a housing association's performance by comparing its performance and business processes with how other similar housing associations are performing. The aim is to demonstrate that performance is among the best and, if not, to learn from what the best performers are doing.

To be of value, comparisons genuinely need to compare like with like, which requires all the organisations to measure performance in the same way and over the same time period. Comparisons also need to take account of the operating context (factors outside an organisation's control) and the degree of difficulty that the organisation faces. For this reason, housing associations often compare themselves with 'peer groups' of similar organisations.

While peer group members then tend to be more comfortable that 'like is being compared with like', and to gain increasing confidence and trust over time about sharing sensitive information, peer group comparison limits the scope for learning if the best performers are not members of the peer group.

Benchmarking works best when organisations use the information as an opportunity to do something better. Where instead of looking for excuses to explain away poor performance (such as the data being out of date), they adopt an open and non-defensive approach and explore what lessons can be learnt from good performers.

Finding out more

Be clear about how performance management reporting is contextualised within your organisation – why you have the indicators you have, how trends over time are depicted, how you compare with peer organisations, and how you compare with sector performance more widely.

D8   How can we ensure value for money?

In brief

The pressure to achieve more with less is ever greater as competition for scarce resources grows. Value for money means ensuring that the organisation is:

- **economic**, by acquiring the required resources (goods, services and staff) as competitively and cost-effectively as possible;

- **efficient**, by producing outputs (homes and services) using the least resources necessary and maximising productivity (doing things in the best way); and

- **effective**, by delivering the desired outcomes (doing the right things).

Efficiency and value for money have been government priorities for some time. Procurement is a key element.

In more detail

Best Value

In 1999, Best Value replaced requirements for local authorities to compulsorily tender services as the method for improving the quality and cost-effectiveness of services.

In 2004, Sir Peter Gershon undertook an independent review of public sector efficiency for the government. His review (the Gershon Report) identified a number of key areas where efficiencies could be found:

- procurement (the process of buying goods and services);

- back office (corporate support services like finance, human resources, payroll, IT, legal, procurement, security and communications);

- transactional services (rents, void efficiencies); and

- productive time (actions that increase productivity like sickness/absence management).

The review defined four ways to improve efficiency:

- reduce inputs for the same outputs – put in fewer resources to get the same result, 'the same for less';

- reduce prices for the same outputs – pay less for inputs to get the same result, also 'the same for less';

- achieve more outputs or improved quality for the same inputs – get better results from the same resources, 'more for the same'; and

- achieve proportionally more outputs or improved quality compared with the extra resources that are used, 'spend more but get even more back'.

The Gershon Report led to CLG introducing efficiency targets across the public sector, and the requirement for housing associations to prepare Annual Efficiency Statements (now incorporated into the annual Self Assessed Compliance Statement). The Tenant Services Authority's Value for Money Standard requires housing associations to have a comprehensive approach to managing resources that provides cost-effective, efficient, quality services.

Strategy

Value for money is a key driver at the heart of providing good quality, cost-effective service delivery. It involves achieving a balance between cost and quality across the 'whole life' of a product, service or building.

A strategic approach to value for money will help to ensure that the organisation achieves as much as possible with its available resources, and is as well equipped as possible to meet customer and stakeholder requirements and expectations. Key aspects of a successful value for money strategy are:

- a clear statement of the organisation's commitment to delivering value for money for tenants as a core aim and value;

- appreciation of the value of adopting a comprehensive economic, efficient and effective approach to resource procurement and management; and to involve a balance of cost, performance and satisfaction measures;

- embedding value for money in the culture of the organisation as an everyday aspect of every staff member's job, encouraging cost-consciousness, developing resource management capacity, and promoting opportunities to make suggestions for savings alongside improvements in service quality;

- harnessing tenant involvement to help identify and prioritise requirements and cost-effective ways of meeting them (eg, how best to deliver a good quality cost-effective response repairs service), alongside promoting opportunities for suggesting savings and improvements in service quality (recognising tenants' keen interest in value for money);

- participating in peer benchmarking opportunities to assess performance and identify areas for improvement as an integral aspect of service review and improvement, eg, performance, repairs costs, management costs, human resource costs (like sickness levels, temporary staff, pay and job evaluation etc.) and, where possible, taking opportunities to compare performance and costs internally between departments or regions;

- using business intelligence to achieve a better understanding of underlying cost drivers and patterns of resource usage by, for instance, reviewing variances in demand for response repairs and investigating particularly high usages, or identifying properties that have particularly high maintenance requirements or refurbishment costs;

- working in partnership to develop initiatives that attract external funding, such as employment training projects for tenants or working with community groups to add value, and joint initiatives with other housing providers locally to improve efficiency and value for money, eg, sharing resources or negotiating service level agreements with housing benefit departments;

- integrating value for money with business planning and service development activities, and with other key strategies like procurement, equality and diversity, risk management, resident involvement, etc; and

- appointing an executive member and a board member as champions to lead on value for money and drive the strategy forward.

Procurement

Good procurement practice plays a key part in improving efficiency and achieving value for money. It can also help to achieve other benefits like economic regeneration and jobs for local people.

All associations should have a clear approach to procurement that outlines how they select, acquire and manage the goods, services and works that they require. Key aspects of effective procurement include:

- a comprehensive strategy that includes all procurement activity, from paper clips to major new building developments;

- specifications that fully embrace diversity and equality, reflect the needs of all tenants, require all contractors to comply with equalities legislation, and permit small ethnic minority businesses to compete;

- involving tenants and capitalising on their experience and ideas, for instance in the choice and management of response repairs and major improvement contractors;

- support for wider sustainability and regeneration objectives, for instance by requiring recycled materials, timber from sustainable sources, or by supporting small and medium-sized enterprises or local training and apprenticeships;

- employing the most appropriate procurement methods, for example, quoting, tendering, partnering, consortium, internal sourcing, e-procurement etc. Many, but not all, housing associations use partnering for repairs contracts: a contractual arrangement where information and risks are shared with contractors to deliver better value for money;

- joining a purchasing consortium and working collaboratively to increase buying power, reduce costs, share skills and market intelligence, and gain access to a wider pool of suppliers. For instance, by joining schemes like Procurement for Housing (a joint initiative between the National Housing Federation, the Chartered Institute of Housing and HouseMark which has more than 700 members) and the London Housing Consortium (for consortium purchasing, procurement frameworks and refurbishment and energy efficiency works);

- compliance with EU procurement rules which require contracts above a certain value to be advertised in the Official Journal of the European Union (OJEU) so as to give all potential suppliers a fair chance of bidding and winning them;

- adopting a detailed annual procurement plan to enable the organisation to manage the procurement process and complete specific procurements in good time, alongside monitoring and reviewing the procurement strategy from time to time. Setting out the likely cycle during the coming two or three years will help both the organisation and potential suppliers to plan ahead;

- ensuring that the risk management system covers the potential failure of significant contracts (typical high risk contracts include response repairs and IT); and

- appointing a senior manager and a board member as procurement champions to promote good procurement practice across the organisation.

Finding out more

Better buys: Improving housing association procurement practice. Audit Commission, 2008: www.audit-commission.gov.uk.

More information about Procurement for Housing is available at www. procurementforhousing.co.uk/home.

More information about London Housing Consortium is available at www.lhc. gov.uk.

Read through your organisation's value for money strategy.

D9 How does external audit work?

In brief

Every housing association is required by law to have an annual financial audit by an independent qualified person or firm of auditors. The external audit provides a safeguard to board members about the financial state of the organisation.

In more detail

External audit

The main purpose of external audit is to check that the organisation's published accounts give a true and fair view of its financial position. It has an important secondary function of providing a management letter which states whether the audit has uncovered any weakness in accounting systems, financial controls, accounting policies and compliance with legislation, regulations and standards.

The annual accounts

The annual accounts present a summary of the organisation's business and financial performance for the previous financial year. Besides outlining income and expenditure, assets and liabilities, and investments and outstanding loans, they also describe the organisation's business activities, governance structure, key financial and investment policies and approach to managing risk.

The requirements are specified by law as interpreted by the UK Accounting Standards Board. A Statement of Recommended Practice (SORP) interprets UK Generally Accepted Accounting Practice (UK GAAP) for registered social housing providers. The SORP is the statement that landlords use in preparing accounts in accordance with applicable accounting standards.

The accounts generally contain a wealth of useful information about an organisation. But it is important to remember that by the time the information is published it is likely to be more than six months out of date.

The role of the audit committee

The audit committee oversees internal and external audit.

Internal audit

Internal audit is a more systematic way of checking that normal managerial processes are working effectively. It will involve a periodic review of all the organisation's control systems. It will test that procedures and policies are being followed and may also include special studies to test value for money. All of these matters will be reported to the board so that appropriate action can be taken. The independence of internal audit arrangements is a particular safeguard for the board.

All organisations need internal audit arrangements. In very small housing associations this may be delegated to an individual board member who carries out periodic checks that delegated activities are being carried out properly. Smaller and medium-sized housing associations may commission external consultants to provide internal audit services, or may be able to appoint a full-time staff member. Some have joined with other similar organisations to share an internal audit service. In large organisations there is likely to be a substantial external contract or an internal audit section whose work is overseen by the audit committee.

Whatever arrangements are made, the board has an overall responsibility to ensure that it is effectively managed. This may be a direct board responsibility in a small organisation or an audit committee in a large one.

Finding out more

A wider role for internal audit, Jane Bloodworth. National Housing Federation, 2004.

Statement of Recommended Practice (SORP): Accounting by registered social housing providers: Update 2010. National Housing Federation, 2010.

Ask for a copy of the association's latest annual accounts and the last management letter.

D10 Can housing associations merge?

In brief

From time to time housing associations come together and create a formal constitutional partnership. This kind of partnership might take the form of a merger (an amalgamation to form a new body), a takeover (where one organisation absorbs the other) or by becoming part of a group structure.

There may be complex legal or tax issues to overcome, especially if one or more of the organisations is a registered charity. It is important to seek legal advice at an early stage.

In more detail

Takeovers and mergers

Typical reasons why housing associations consider merging are:

- to reduce costs and become more efficient, eg, by sharing or making better use of resources or by achieving scale advantages, particularly for procurement;

- to achieve a particular strategy, eg, to strengthen ability to compete for investment funds or to gain investment partner status with the Homes and Communities Agency;

- to strengthen market position, eg, to gain access to new markets, achieve stock rationalisation or take advantage of synergies between organisations; or

- as a way of surviving a calamitously adverse situation.

Housing associations are not like profit-making companies. They do not distribute profits to shareholders and shareholders cannot sell their shares. It is therefore not possible for one association to 'take over' another by buying its shares. Shareholders have to agree to any change in constitutional structure.

The proposed link up may also require consent from the Tenant Services Authority or the Charity Commission. A merger between charities is only possible if both charities have compatible objects.

'Merger' is usually thought of as the coming together of two similar organisations to create a new organisation. If one is much larger or more dominant in some way than the other, then a merger will often be described as a 'takeover'. For housing associations, this usually means that one organisation's board members or senior staff, or culture or way of doing things, becomes predominant and, in effect, takes over.

The role of the board

While it is the shareholding membership that will make any final decision, board members are the guardians of the housing association's mission and play a central role in any consideration of the organisation's future. The first, and most important, step is for the board to consider carefully the rationale for amalgamating (the reasons for change) and be satisfied that merger is the right way forward for the organisation (and not other possible ways forward). Board members must base their decision on what is best for the organisation.

Having made an 'in principle' decision to explore partnership options further, the board's role is to lead the process. This will involve agreeing the framework for negotiations, supervising the process, taking all material decisions, and planning and implementing the post-amalgamation leadership and governance arrangements. Often a small group of members is appointed to take matters forward on behalf of the board, in conjunction with external advisers. An outline of the process is:

- explore and evaluate different partnership options, including the legal and regulatory implications, and decide a preferred option;

- identify a merger partner (possibly by advertising), undertake detailed negotiations and reach an 'in principle' agreement;

- establish and take account of the views of tenants and other key stakeholders;

- undertake a 'due diligence' investigation of the assets, liabilities and risks that are to be taken on to ensure that each party has a true and fair picture of the other and to minimise the chances of encountering unforeseen surprises after it is too late to back out;

- take a final decision to proceed (or not); and

- execute the formal legal process of bringing the two or more separate legal entities together into one organisation.

Alongside the formal amalgamation process, the board will also need to plan and implement the future leadership and governance arrangements. At any stage board members may feel the need to pause and reconsider whether partnership is the right way forward.

Why some work and some fail

It is very important to understand the rationale for amalgamating – the reasons for change and why merger is the right solution for both organisations. If the rationale is not clear, or they are not compatible or mutually beneficial, then it is much less likely that a merger will be successful.

Some of the factors that are likely to influence the success of a merger are:

- a mutually beneficial arrangement: the board members and senior executives of both parties clearly understand and are comfortable with each other's rationale for amalgamating and the agreed way forward. If some are unhappy, or feel it is a shotgun marriage, there needs to be a clear process for speedily eliminating any resistance;

- stakeholder involvement: tenants and other key stakeholders are kept fully informed about the changes and their views are taken into account;

- focus: maintaining focus on good service delivery and not allowing the merger to become the focus of attention at the expense of continuing to deliver a good service. Checking that any planned service improvements are actually delivered;

- vision and culture: a shared ethos and shared values and norms are very important. Continuing worries about job security, or a lingering 'us and them' attitude between two staff groups, can have a detrimental effect on service delivery. A clear vision for the new organisation, and regular updates, will help staff to adjust and feel a part of the new organisation;

- speedy implementation: having a common way of working in place from day one (culture, letterheads, answering the phone etc.) will maximise the chances of success;

- purpose: monitoring the outcomes and, if the benefits are not achieved as planned, seeking to understand why and put a plan in place to remedy the situation.

Cultural differences can be one of the biggest obstacles to overcome when organisations try to merge. When mergers fail, people often point to issues such as identity, communication problems, human resources problems, ego clashes, and inter-group conflicts. Successful mergers require the board and senior staff to be cultural leaders facilitating the change from two old cultures into one new culture.

Finding out more

Groups, mergers and alliances, KPMG LLP, National Housing Federation, 2007.

D11 When does the board need external advice?

In brief

Boards should seek and take independent external advice for major financial decisions, new ventures or other areas of high risk. It can also be valuable to get an external perspective on such issues as senior management pay.

In more detail

Boards have a right to expect competent advice from their staff. They also have a duty to consider and challenge such advice. While external advice does not always have to be taken, the board must feel free to do so on matters of importance. The ability to take external advice on any subject from an independent source is a key protection for board members, irrespective of the size of the organisation. It should not be viewed by the board or staff as showing a lack of confidence in either party. For some charities, taking advice is a statutory requirement in relation to certain investments or borrowings.

All such advice should be sought on the basis of a written appointment and an agreed basis of charging. Typical situations in which a board might seek external assistance would be:

- if a change in structure is being considered – for example, a consolidation of a group structure or a union with another organisation – and how this might best be effected;

- advice on tax or pensions;

- advice on remuneration (for instance for board members or for the chief executive).

Finding out more

It may be helpful to find out when your organisation last sought external advice and why.

Looking outwards

Successful organisations are outward looking, alert to the wider environment, and ready to learn from others. Housing associations are no different, and the board, in its leadership role, needs to maintain an external focus. This chapter is about the relationships boards and board members need to have, and how to make them effective.

E1   How can I be an ambassador?
In brief

All board members are ambassadors for their housing association. Being an ambassador means always taking care to present the organisation in a positive light and to promote its interests. This involves supporting the association's policies and board decisions, and behaving courteously and abiding by the code of conduct at all times.

'Ambassador' is not the same as 'authorised spokesperson'. As part of a communications framework, each board should agree who is authorised to speak on the organisation's behalf. In most cases this will be the chief executive or the chair.

In more detail

In whatever setting board members find themselves, they will always be seen by others as a representative of the organisation. Being an ambassador means being mindful of how other people outside the organisation might regard you and interpret what you say. It is a role that comes with the appointment and cannot be sidestepped or ignored. Even after resigning there will be a duty to avoid disclosing confidential information.

In any contact with third parties, board members must always support the housing association's policies and board decisions, and not disclose any disagreements or dissent. If a board member has a serious concern about the propriety of any actions by the housing association or any individual within it or with whom it has dealings, and the matter cannot be satisfactorily resolved through normal procedures, the board member should use the housing association's whistle blowing procedure or, in accordance with the Public Interest Disclosure Act 1998, notify the Tenant Services Authority or other designated body under the Act.

> ### Finding out more
> Read your organisation's code of conduct so that you have a firm understanding of the protocol around external events.

E2   How should board members relate to tenants?
In brief

Tenants are key stakeholders. Every housing association should be engaging effectively with tenants to understand their full range of views, opinions and needs, and their satisfaction with services, both individually and as a group. These arrangements should include ways for board members to relate to tenants as a group, and will often involve regular joint meetings with tenant representatives or with a tenant forum or tenant panel. Programmes of visits to housing schemes and projects from time to time provide excellent opportunities for board members to meet individual tenants.

At a personal level, board members should always behave politely and respectfully towards tenants and listen sympathetically to what they have to say, but try to avoid cutting across accountability lines or getting involved in the detail of individual cases.

In more detail

A collaborative partnership

Traditionally, tenants did not have much say in what services were provided or how they were provided. Co-regulation introduces a new partnership approach, with landlords and tenants working together locally to improve services. Boards are now firmly responsible for effective service delivery, and accountable to tenants, not the regulator, for service delivery performance. Board members should be seeking to develop collaborative working partnerships with tenants which give genuine opportunities to influence strategic priorities, housing-related policies and services, and to scrutinise performance.

Relationships between board members and individual tenants

Board members should always seek to embody the values of the organisation, and to demonstrate and reinforce how tenants are central to everything that the housing association does. The scope and frequency of contact between board members and tenants will depend, to a large extent, on the size and type of the organisation and its culture and practice. In larger housing associations board members tend to have only limited contact with tenants, whereas in smaller associations and co-operatives there is likely to be much more regular contact.

If a matter is raised with a board member individually, the appropriate response is usually to refer the matter to the staff member responsible, and to explain to the tenant what will happen next, thank them for raising the matter, and then take time later to check that it has been satisfactorily dealt with.

Board members must take care not to be seen to be advocating on a tenant's behalf, or special pleading or asking for an exception to be made. If the housing association's response does not seem appropriate for the tenant's circumstances, then the matter ought to be addressed in the same way that any other similar issue would be. This may involve using the complaints procedure or via a policy review or continuous improvement process.

Tenant board members

Board members who are tenants are very likely to have much more regular contact with other tenants in the area where they live. Where difficult decisions are made, there should be a clear communications strategy regarding how messages are delivered 'on the ground'. Boards must not expect tenant board members to be the channel for tenant views. While tenant board members provide valuable insights into the organisation's services, and help boards to be aware of the impact of their decisions on tenants, they do not speak on behalf of tenants and should not be a substitute for more systematic involvement. The whole board needs to have mechanisms for relating to the whole tenant group.

Finding out more

Section G1 gives more detail about how the partnership with tenants should work.

E3   How should board members relate to the wider staff team?
In brief

Outside formal governance structures and procedures, the relationship with the wider staff team is usually ambassadorial in nature. Board members should always strive to be warm and friendly and approach tasks collaboratively. At the same time board members cannot escape their formal position and should always be seeking to embody and reinforce the values of the organisation, support its strategies and policies, and back up the executive's position.

In more detail

All board members have a direct relationship with the chief executive and other senior staff. Other staff may also attend committee meetings or participate in working groups with board members. The organisation should also have agreed arrangements and procedures for negotiating about terms and conditions and dealing with other staffing matters.

The scope and frequency of contact between board members and the wider staff team will depend, to a large extent, on the size of the organisation and its culture and practice. In some housing associations board members have only limited contact with the wider staff team, in others there is much more regular contact.

Whenever interacting with staff, board members should be warm and friendly and listen sympathetically to what staff have to say and, if it is appropriate, take the opportunity to appreciate the key role that staff play in delivering high quality outcomes for tenants. But board members must also take care not to do or say anything that might undermine managers or the line management structure. If the setting is task-oriented, board members should seek to work collaboratively and in partnership with staff and avoid, as far as possible, telling staff what to do.

In interactions with staff about individual tenant matters, board members must take care not to be seen to be advocating on a tenant's behalf or special pleading or asking for an exception to be made, or attempting to give instructions that cut across formal accountability lines.

E4   How should the board work with the regulator?

In brief

Housing associations should regard the regulator as a critical friend. The board should aim to have an open and constructive relationship with the regulator's staff, and adopt a 'comply or explain' approach to meeting their requirements. If the association encounters serious problems or difficulties, the board should be open and honest about them with the regulator, with a view to agreeing steps that the association will take to overcome the difficulties.

In more detail

Normal liaison

Regulation may seem irksome, and is rarely perfect in execution, but it should be recognised as an essential feature of providing core services to the community with the benefit of public funds. It is also a protection for the key role that housing associations play in delivering social housing. Public subsidy rests ultimately on public consent.

Board members need to understand and keep up to date with the regulator's requirements and their implications for the housing association. The chief executive and other senior managers should, as part of their role, keep the board informed about the regulator's requirements and make sure that policies, procedures and other arrangements comply with them. However, the board is ultimately responsible for compliance.

The regulator's aims are to ensure that tenants receive a fair deal and to protect public and private investment. Its requirements are generally based on sound management principles and good professional practice. If, for some reason, these requirements appear to be overly onerous, prescriptive or inappropriate for a housing association's business or circumstances, a constructive approach is to seek to demonstrate how the organisation meets the regulator's requirements in a way that is appropriate to the organisation.

For those who provide high levels of care and support, there can be additional areas of regulation. Particular responsibilities also arise for registered homes and other forms of specialist care.

Being in supervision

If a housing association fails to meet required standards or gets into financial or management difficulties, the Tenant Services Authority may take regulatory action. Except where there are pressing reasons to take immediate action, the regulator will generally expect housing associations to take steps to self-improve. It has a range of enforcement powers which include appointing new members to strengthen the board and removing board members. If required, the regulator can ask the Homes and Communities Agency to suspend funding, and it also has powers to direct the association to transfer its stock.

The voluntary undertaking

A housing association facing the prospect of greater scrutiny or enforcement action can be required to give a voluntary undertaking to pursue a course of action to remedy the situation, which the regulator must take into account in deciding what further action, if any, to take.

Finding out more

The regulatory framework for social housing in England from April 2010.
Tenant Services Authority, 2010.

E5   How should we work with local authorities?
In brief

Housing associations work in partnership with local authorities and contribute to meeting housing need and creating sustainable communities. The board should ensure that the association maintains constructive relationships with the main local authorities in whose areas the organisation works.

In more detail

Local authorities are responsible for taking a strategic overview of the housing and support needs of people living in their area. Local authorities also have statutory responsibilities for housing people who are homeless or inadequately housed. For most housing associations, local authorities are their most important partner.

Where an organisation has a substantial presence and is a key provider, there should be clear arrangements for regular liaison on key matters of mutual interest (if appropriate, backed up by written agreements) including:

- nominations, allocations and lettings (often a common or unified approach);

- future development plans;

- tackling key issues like antisocial behaviour or employment and training;

- meeting tenants' support needs and safeguarding;

- housing benefit payment; and

- annual information to be published.

Sometimes partnership work will also be conducted through formal groupings, such as Local Strategic Partnerships, bringing together other kinds of service providers (eg, health, policing).

Finding out more

Find out if your association participates in any formal meetings with one or more local authorities, who attends and what kind of business is discussed.

E6   What do lenders expect from the board?

In brief

Lenders will want to be assured that the housing association is financially viable and continuing to meet its commitments and covenants to lenders, and that the board understands the business and is being prudent and not taking any undue risks. They will also want to be reassured that reports match the reality of what is happening on the ground and that governance is functioning properly.

In more detail

Most housing association loans are long term, often for 25 years or more. Lenders have an interest in protecting the security of their loans and ensuring that borrowers are able to meet the repayment terms and comply with any covenants throughout the life of the loan. Sometimes covenants can be onerous, particularly if a housing association has borrowed from many different lenders, and care must be taken to ensure that an action does not inadvertently breach a covenant.

Accountability to lenders is contractual through loan agreements which usually contain formal reporting requirements. However, it is a good idea to maintain an ongoing dialogue and to alert lenders in advance if any potential difficulties are foreseen. Providing boards act prudently and reasonably, lenders are usually also reasonable.

Finding out more

Speak to your organisation's finance director (or equivalent) and find out how much money the organisation has borrowed, and from which lenders. Ask how often the lender meets with board members, and what is discussed.

E7 Should we be in touch with the wider housing sector?

In brief

There is a great deal that housing associations can learn from each other, and a great deal to be gained by coming together to share information and to lobby and campaign on matters of mutual interest. The National Housing Federation provides many forums for sharing experience and good practice, and a national voice for the sector. There are particular opportunities for board members to meet and share experiences.

In more detail

There are many practical benefits to working collaboratively with other housing associations through forums, federations or consortia, whether focused on sharing costs or on sharing knowledge and learning, or both. (See D7 for information on the benefits of benchmarking.)

Whether board members are meeting formally or informally with other organisations, the value of looking outwards in this way appears to have a strong correlation with improvement.

Challenges and concerns are often common across the sector, and benefit from considered discussion. Among the kinds of activities you might consider are:

- formal participation in a consortium, federation or forum;

- participating in joint training and/or strategy sessions;

- observing a board meeting in another organisation;

- attending conferences, briefings, talks, open days; or

- forming a group for chairs of associations in your local area.

Finding out more

Ask the chair or chief executive about the association's formal membership of any local groups.

Check with the company secretary what other kinds of networking may be available to you.

Chapter F

The board as a landlord

Landlord services or 'housing services' are the services that have the most effect on, and are of the greatest importance to, tenants and other residents. Yet in the past many housing associations, with the best of intentions, tended to focus on providing additional housing, and to place less emphasis on the quality of service to tenants or on listening to what tenants actually want. The inspection process has set standards for service delivery and given clear incentives to improve the quality of services.

Housing services need to be seen in a wider context. Large estates may have poor access to schools and shops or inadequate recreation facilities. The local community may have a high rate of unemployment and consequently a dependence on state benefits for its income. There may be problems of antisocial behaviour, vandalism and other forms of crime including drug dealing. In such situations, a narrow focus on housing services may well fail, where a broader community partnership approach will succeed.

Historically, housing associations have been required to focus on housing those in greatest need to the exclusion of all other factors. This has sometimes led to concentrations of poverty that have then contributed to a cycle of decline. There is now wide acceptance that mixed communities are more likely to be sustainable communities, and these are now seen as a key target in area regeneration programmes. There is also a strong desire to give prospective tenants more choice – even in areas of higher demand.

The quality of service outcomes and the active involvement of tenants are central to the Tenant Services Authority's co-regulatory approach. Housing associations are expected to work in partnership with their tenants. The goal is to ensure that in future housing associations provide services that are sensitive to, and meet, the full range of tenants' and residents' differing requirements and desire for choice.

F1 What are the board's legal responsibilities as a landlord?

In brief

The board is responsible for ensuring that the housing association meets all legal and regulatory requirements relating to its role as landlord. These include nomination commitments, the form of tenancy, security of tenure, rent levels, gas servicing, disrepair, health and safety, equality and diversity, and obligations relating to enforcing tenant commitments on antisocial behaviour.

In more detail

Allocations

Housing associations are expected to assist local authorities with their homelessness duties, and by housing people nominated by the local authority. Nominations are normally under formal nomination agreements which were entered into at the time the housing was developed or transferred, and which set out the local authority's rights to nominate tenants to an agreed proportion of the homes. Local housing authorities generally have at least 50 per cent nomination rights and this can increase to 100 per cent if the local authority has made a substantial contribution (such as providing free land). It is increasingly common for housing associations to pool resources with each other and a local authority and maintain a common register as part of a choice-based lettings scheme. This means that prospective tenants only have to complete one application form. Whether the waiting list is the housing association's own or is shared with others, it is still for each organisation to take the key decisions as to whom should be housed.

Tenancy responsibilities

All housing associations must comply with all statutory and legal requirements governing the operation of the various forms of tenancy or occupancy agreement that the association uses. They are expected to offer the most secure form of tenure compatible with the purpose of the housing and the sustainability of the community. Other aspects are explored below.

Finding out more

Request a briefing from the company secretary about your legal responsibilities.

F2   What rights and obligations do tenants have?

In brief

The rights and obligations of both tenants and landlord are set out in the tenancy agreement. Tenants' rights will include security of tenure, rights to repairs, succession and to make improvements and, for post-1996 tenancies, the right to acquire.

The tenancy agreement will include tenants' obligations to pay rent, keep their home in reasonable condition and not to behave in an antisocial manner towards other tenants. It will also include the housing association's obligation to provide the tenant with repairs and other services.

In more detail

Tenants' rights are either statutory (guaranteed by law) or contractual (guaranteed through the tenancy agreement). It is good practice for tenancy agreements to go beyond the minimum required by legislation. The tenant's rights will include those set out in the regulator's National Standards. European law requires that the agreement should be in plain English. Further advice and guidance will be set out in the housing association's tenants' handbook. This will include, among other things, the organisation's complaints procedure and the right to take complaints to the Housing Ombudsman if complaints are not dealt with fairly.

Many housing associations now offer new tenants fixed period 'starter' tenancies. Provided the tenants abide by the terms and conditions during this probationary period, these tenancies then become long-term tenancies.

Tenants who became tenants before the implementation of the Housing Act 1988 are often referred to as 'secure' or 'fair rent' tenants. Secure tenants of non-charitable housing associations have the right to buy their home at a discount. Post-Housing Act 1996 tenants have the right to acquire. Tenants who do not have the right to buy or the right to acquire are likely to be eligible to apply for a grant to help them buy a home on the open market, thus freeing up current tenanted accommodation. The availability of the grants is limited. Both charitable and non-charitable associations may also have voluntary sales programmes.

There are several different forms of tenancy, and also different types of agreement for other occupiers. The continuing trend of transfers from local authorities to housing associations is adding to the pressure to have a single form of social housing tenancy that is common to both sectors.

Finding out more

Landlord and tenant a practical guide for social landlords, John Bryant.
National Housing Federation, 1998.

F3 How should rents and service charges be set?

In brief

Rents are every landlord's main source of income. The government sets target rents for
the main sizes of accommodation at levels that reflect property values and average manual
earnings in different parts of the country. There are proposals to change the system and allow
housing associations to charge rents closer to market levels.

Where associations provide additional services like heating, cleaning or landscaping, there is
generally an additional service charge to cover the cost. Service charges can be fixed or variable.

In more detail

Setting rents

The way in which rents are set, increased and collected matters greatly to the organisation
and its tenants. Housing associations are under conflicting pressures to keep rents affordable
(particularly for people in low-paid employment) and to increase them in order to strengthen
their financial position and capacity to develop new housing. With so many housing association
tenants eligible for housing benefit, the government also takes a keen interest.

Until 1988, most housing associations charged 'fair rents' set by the government rent officer
service rather than by the association. New lettings after 1988 have been on what are generally
referred to as 'assured rents', which are set by the association. Most associations therefore have
a two-tier rent structure in which identical properties can be let on differing rents. Associations
managing transferred local authority housing may also have a two-tier rent structure, with new
tenants post-transfer typically paying higher assured tenancy rents.

In 2002 the government introduced a new rent policy designed to restructure rents and
achieve a rational basis for rent levels across the social housing sector by 2012. Most housing
associations now charge rents that match, or are close to, target rent levels. The government
now is proposing to introduce a new rent policy which will allow developing housing
associations to charge up to 80 per cent of market rent levels on new homes and on some re-

lettings. This flexibility will only be available to those associations that can demonstrate their future commitment to developing new homes (a 'something for something' offer, ie, flexibility of rent setting in exchange for new supply).

Service charges

Where housing associations provide additional services, there is generally a service charge in addition to the rent. Leaseholders who receive services also pay a service charge. Service charges can be substantial. Housing associations are required to account fairly for service costs, and tenants and leaseholders have the right to see service charge accounts. While organisations can include a reasonable administration charge, they cannot charge more than the service is worth. Housing associations sometimes have difficulty in making sure that all service costs are covered by service charge income.

Finding out more

Service charges: A guide for housing associations (4th edition). D. Rawson. National Housing Federation, 2010.

F4   What do I need to know about repairs and maintenance?
In brief

Repairs and maintenance is the service that most tenants most value. From the housing association's point of view, it is also protection of a key asset. Both aspects are crucial.

Planning the best use of maintenance resources involves adopting a prudent approach that strikes an appropriate balance between responsive (or day-to-day) repairs, planned repairs and value for money. It will include day-to-day repairs, cyclical repairs (painting and gas servicing etc.), planned and capital works, works on empty properties and property adaptations.

The long-term impact on the environment of decisions about asset management should also inform the board's approach to decisions in this area.

In more detail

The effectiveness of maintenance arrangements (including gas servicing) and asset management is now subject to detailed scrutiny.

Tenants generally want clarity about what the repairs service covers and the standards to expect, a speedy response (for emergency and urgent repairs), a choice of appointment time, work completed to a good standard and value for money. Response times are now a key performance indicator across the sector and all associations should be able to meet them in well over 90 per cent of cases.

Properties should also meet modern design and quality standards and health and safety requirements. Associations are required to ensure that all their properties meet the government's Decent Homes Standard. This standard includes modern facilities and services, good thermal insulation and heating and a good state of general repair. Many housing associations have had to modify their asset management strategy to comply with the standard.

From the organisation's perspective it will be essential to get good value for money for expenditure on repairs. While responsive maintenance is always a priority, well run organisations try to spend a higher proportion of their resources on planned and cyclical maintenance so that the property is serviced rather than being left until a fault is reported. This approach has safety advantages, and is essential for gas appliances. Maintenance may also be required when tenants vacate a flat. This can delay re-letting and is often a cause of rent loss (usually called void loss). Poor liaison between housing management and maintenance staff can increase such losses.

Housing associations now have to make provisions for replacement of major components such as kitchens, roofs, wiring and other elements on a cyclical basis. Well run organisations will carry out periodic stock condition surveys of their whole stock. They will maintain a comprehensive database of the building elements in the stock and use this to plan for long-term expenditure by forecasting on the basis of their expected life cycles. The resulting expenditure forecasts will be an important element in long-term financial projections. Regular inspection will enable judgements to be made about whether to bring forward or delay works and this will inform the more detailed plans for the next few years.

It is important for the effective use of maintenance resources to have effective procurement. Traditionally this would be based around a good panel of contractors, effective tendering and pricing arrangements and a system of pre- and post-inspections that vary according to the type and value of work. More recently, larger associations have developed partnering arrangements with maintenance contractors. Some also have direct labour organisations. Now that effective procurement is a major thrust of government policy there have been a number of further initiatives. These include multi-association procurement groups that are achieving significant volume procurement savings.

It is important to have an effective system of tracking maintenance requests and the consequent works orders. Computerisation can make a substantial difference and is essential for both medium-sized and larger organisations. Those with a regional or area structure can compare costs between regions and use this to spot trends, spread good practice and inhibit inefficiency.

Finally, effective asset management will be key to improving the energy and carbon efficiency of all housing stock if housing associations are to play their part in meeting the government's CO_2 2050 targets. Asset management strategies need to take account of how the energy and carbon efficiency of existing homes is improved as part of planned maintenance and improvement programmes. With fuel poverty a growing problem, helping tenants to understand how to use their homes and to benefit from any energy efficiency improvements is also an important priority.

Finding out more

Read your organisation's asset management strategy.

F5   Why does equality and diversity matter?

In brief

Housing associations exist to serve the whole community. Equality of opportunity and appreciating and valuing diversity are central to enabling everyone to participate fully. It is essential that housing associations treat everyone fairly and with respect and do not discriminate unlawfully, however unintentionally. This is especially important for vulnerable people and others who are less able to take care of themselves.

Equality and diversity issues affect everyone at some point in their lives. Housing associations also need to understand and respond to the particular needs of tenants, and demonstrate how they have taken into account the needs of tenants across all the different equality strands (more information on these follows below).

In more detail

Being fair and inclusive

Communities are made up of people from different backgrounds and experiences. All housing associations should be seeking to:

- be accessible to all parts of the community;

- enable everyone to participate fully and overcome the barriers that stop people doing so;

- provide the right range of services to meet tenants' differing needs and requirements;

- promote understanding and good relations between tenants with different backgrounds and experiences; and

- harness and recruit the best talent.

Yet prejudice and discrimination can lead to some people being treated unfairly or excluded, however unintentionally. Discrimination can arise through not being aware of the distinctive needs of different groups. It can arise if the association does not go out of its way to publicise access to its housing in a way that reaches all parts of the community.

It is important that associations practise what they preach in the way that they manage their work and employ staff. Particular care must be taken to avoid discrimination in the provision of housing and other services and to ensure compliance with the Equality Act 2010. The Act offers protection from discrimination, harassment and victimisation to people affected by nine protected characteristics. There are the 'big six' that many may already be familiar with – age, disability, race, religion or belief, sex, and sexual orientation – and three others that are derived from the Sex Discrimination Act 1975 (gender reassignment, marriage and civil partnership, pregnancy and maternity). It is illegal to treat one person less favourably than another because of a protected characteristic when providing goods, facilities and services and employing staff.

Equality means ensuring that everyone has equal opportunity to participate, contribute to and benefit from the housing and services that a housing association provides. It encompasses the policies and steps required to eliminate discrimination and ensure everyone is treated fairly and respectfully. Equality does not mean treating everyone the same. It means empowering people to fulfil their ambitions, to be themselves, and to be different, if they wish.

Diversity recognises and appreciates the benefits that people's differences and talents bring to an organisation or community. Together, equality and diversity combine equal opportunity to participate with respecting and catering for people's differences. The aim is for everyone to feel included and valued.

Monitoring and insight
Confidential, user-friendly monitoring helps to ensure that services are open to everyone and that applicants and tenants are treated fairly and that no-one is discriminated against

unlawfully. Monitoring also helps to create a more inclusive community by demonstrating that the organisation values diversity.

While monitoring is principally concerned with performance, over time it also helps to reveal the scale of need. This aspect dovetails with and supplements customer insight, understanding who the organisation's customers are and what they want.

The Tenant Services Authority requires housing associations to understand and take account of tenants' different needs across all the equality strands. Some characteristics, such as sexuality and gender identity, are very sensitive. These are by no means the only characteristics that are sensitive, but they are ones that many people know very little, if anything, about. So a good place to start is to encourage greater awareness about and sensitivity to less familiar protected characteristics.

Finding out more

Equality and diversity: A framework for review and action, J. Jeffery and Seager, R. National Housing Federation, 2006.

Equality Act 2010 Guidance for service providers: What equality law means for your voluntary and community sector organisation (including charities and religion or belief organisations). Equality and Human Rights Commission, 2010: www.equalityhumanrights.com.

Equality, Diversity and Good Relations in Housing. Chartered Institute of Housing, 2009: www.cih.org.

F6   How should we deal with antisocial behaviour?

In brief

Housing associations, along with local authorities, the police and other agencies have a key role to play in tackling antisocial behaviour and creating safe and sustainable communities. Action requires a balanced approach between prevention, early intervention, support and enforcement.

In more detail

Antisocial behaviour (ASB) is any aggressive, intimidating or destructive activity that damages or destroys another person's quality of life. This kind of behaviour can seriously affect the quality of life for tenants and have a negative impact on neighbourhoods and communities. The

Tenant Services Authority expects providers to work in partnership with other public agencies to prevent and tackle ASB in the neighbourhoods where they own property.

Housing associations have been and remain committed to tackling ASB, not only in terms of enforcing good behaviour but also through prevention, early intervention and support. They continue to develop a range of housing management, community safety and regeneration initiatives in order to do this, often involving and relying upon other partners like Community Safety Partnerships to achieve the best outcomes for all concerned.

Prevention activities include setting clear tenancy conditions, using starter tenancies, responding quickly to environmental problems, good neighbour agreements, neighbourhood warden schemes and diversionary activities for young people. Early intervention includes mediation and acceptable behaviour contracts (ABCs). Support includes helping perpetrators to change behaviour, family intervention and safeguarding vulnerable individuals. Where enforcement action is necessary, there is now a wide range of powers that housing associations and their partners can use to tackle ASB.

Finding out more

Tackling anti-social behaviour: Tools and powers – toolkit for social landlords. CLG, 2010: available as a free download from www.communities. gov.uk/publications/housing/toolspowersguide.

The CIH ASB Action Team offers advice, guidance and good practice, see www.cih.org/asbactionteam.

Reporting antisocial behaviour: Directgov website: www.direct.gov.uk/en/ CrimeJusticeAndTheLaw/Reportingcrimeandantisocialbehaviour.

F7   What do I need to know about inspection?
In brief

The purpose of external inspection is to drive up service standards. Inspectors assess performance against a published set of criteria known as Key Lines of Enquiry (KLOE) and make two judgements: how good is the service and how likely it is to improve.

Inspection should in future be an unusual event. The government has announced plans to limit consumer regulation to serious failure. Inspection remains as an investigatory tool but will no longer be routine. If the regulator suspects a housing association is failing to meet its standards, it will discuss its concerns with the association first and take account of the approach to self-improvement before deciding whether to commission an inspection.

In more detail

The inspection process focuses on the quality of services delivered to residents. Inspection reports provide an independent assessment of service delivery outcomes and this can have an important influence on the reputation of an organisation. A positive report enhances an association's reputation while an adverse one is damaging. Inspection outcomes inform regulatory action by the Tenant Services Authority.

Currently the Housing Inspectorate carries out inspections on behalf of the Tenant Services Authority. The Inspectorate is part of the Audit Commission, which the government plans to abolish in 2012. Inspections may in future be commissioned from independent providers.

Finding out more

Transitional arrangements for the inspection of registered social housing providers: Joint statement by the TSA and Audit Commission, November 2010: www.tenantservicesauthority.org.

F8   What does 'continuous improvement' mean?

In brief

Continuous improvement focuses on using feedback and suggestions for eliminating inefficiencies to make incremental improvements in services over time. A commitment to continuous improvement is central to delivering a quality service.

In more detail

Continuous improvement involves promoting a learning culture throughout the organisation which welcomes feedback and suggestions, views mistakes and errors as an opportunity to learn lessons, and then uses the information to continuously improve services.

Continuous improvement is a key feature of the way all quality management systems work. It is an alternative to making major process changes (like buying a new computer system). Small improvements are easier to implement. Involving staff in improving performance encourages them to take ownership of their work, reinforces team working and improves motivation.

> ### Finding out more
>
> *Better than before: the improvement journey*, Campbell Tickell. Tenant Services Authority, 2010: www.tenantservicesauthority.org.
>
> *Making it work: Approaches to improving service delivery*, Trimmer CS. National Housing Federation, 2006.

F9   Is it worth getting quality marks and accreditations?

In brief

Quality marks and accreditations are business techniques for improving the quality and consistency of services. It is important to choose the approach that best fits the organisation's circumstances so as to maximise the gain from the investment in time and resources.

In more detail

Quality systems

The purpose of having a quality system is to ensure that customers' requirements are met first time, on time, every time. The benefit to the customer is high satisfaction with services and the comfort of knowing that their requirements will be met consistently. The benefit to the organisation is avoiding the consequences and costs of making mistakes (having to spend time putting things right and dealing with complaints, damage to reputation, loss of future work etc.).

The organisation can implement quality management techniques on its own or by means of one of the externally verified routes. The former can be more closely tailored to the organisation's particular circumstances. The latter provides the discipline of external assessment and the promotional benefit of accreditation (a quality kitemark), which can be useful when bidding for contracts.

QHS, Charter Mark, ISO 9001 etc.

Housing associations are increasingly using established techniques and systems for improving the quality and consistency of services. These include the European Business Excellence Model, Charter Mark, ISO 9001, Investors in People, Investors in Excellence, Total Quality Management, and others.

Most of these approaches concentrate on establishing good practice, incorporating it into clear procedures and then setting up mechanisms to ensure that they are being implemented. Some focus on the quality of staff and leadership, others more on processes and systems. The target of promoting quality is usually a more effective mechanism for motivating compliance with policies and procedures than the fear of being found out by an internal auditor.

Finding out more

EFQM Shares what works. EFQM, 2010: www.efqm.org.

F10 What does the Housing Ombudsman do?

In brief

The Housing Ombudsman Service investigates housing association tenants' complaints if a tenant isn't satisfied with the landlord's final response. If the Ombudsman finds maladministration, he or she can require the association to put things right.

In more detail

The complaints process

Occasionally things do go wrong and services do break down. Sometimes organisations fail to fully understand or fully respond to a tenant's particular situation or circumstances, or to fulfil their expectations. Complaints offer an opportunity to put right something that has gone wrong, and also provide free feedback about service quality.

Complaints processes often have three stages: front line resolution, review and appeal. Sometimes there is an 'informal' stage to enable staff to focus on immediate resolution and avoid wasting time wondering 'is this a query or a complaint?' The review stage should be performed by senior staff who are not routinely involved in the service and able to take a fresh look (ie, director or chief executive level). The appeal stage should be the best possible attempt to resolve matters on behalf of the organisation.

The best complaints systems make it easy to complain, aim to resolve the complaint to the complainant's satisfaction as quickly as possible, and then to learn any lessons about gaps or shortcomings and how the organisation can improve services in future. This usually requires a problem-solving approach that treats each case on its own merits and allows staff to exercise some discretion, in line with the organisation's values and overall approach to customer service, accompanied by a complaints handling system that ensures speedy responses and captures the issues and lessons for the organisation.

The role of board members

The board sets the overall approach to handling complaints and agrees the complaints procedure and compensation arrangements. The final appeal stage often involves a panel of board members who hear appeals.

The appeal stage should only come into play after the best efforts of executive staff have been unable to resolve the complaint. While it will be important to establish that staff behaved courteously, followed the organisation's policies and procedures, and complied with the law and regulatory requirements, it is particularly important that board members adopt an open-minded and non-defensive approach and focus on making the best attempt to agree an outcome that is fair and reasonable in all the circumstances.

The role of the Ombudsman

The Housing Ombudsman Service is set up by law to investigate housing association tenants' complaints. All housing associations that are registered providers must be members. Other landlords can join voluntarily. The Ombudsman looks at complaints after the final stage of the landlord's complaints procedure. He or she is required to establish what is fair in all the circumstances, and generally encourages a conciliatory approach. If maladministration is found, the Ombudsman can make orders or recommendations to put things right. The Tenant Services Authority enforces decisions, if required. Generally housing associations accept the Ombudsman's findings.

Learning from complaints

Complaints are an important source of information about what is not working well. From time to time the board should expect to receive reports about complaints performance, for example, the type and volume of informal and formal complaints, and levels of satisfaction with their resolution and with the process. The board will need to satisfy itself that the organisation uses this information to learn lessons, both for services and for how complaints are handled.

Finding out more

Information about the Housing Ombudsman is available at www.housing-ombudsman.org.uk.

You may find it helpful to familiarise yourself with the type and volume of complaints by reading the last complaints report to the board.

F11 What about tenants with special needs?
In brief

The housing association sector has always played an active role in providing supported housing and care for people with special needs. Over a third of the overall turnover for the sector, and well over half of all staff employed are concerned with supported housing and care.

Approaches that support independent living and provide care that is tailored to each individual's needs are increasingly favoured over more traditional institutional settings. As the personalisation of adult social care develops, individuals will increasingly have personal budgets to purchase their own support, a move that is likely to lead to fundamental changes in the demand for care and support services.

In more detail
What are special needs?

The Tenant Services Authority expects housing associations to demonstrate that they understand and are responding to the needs of tenants with additional support needs.

Older people and frail older people are the largest group, but there are also substantial services to people with learning disabilities or mental ill health, and people with various dependency problems. One of the characteristics of this area is the wide range of different needs that can require special care and the fact that many people have multiple needs which do not fit into neat categories.

There is an increasing demand for housing with care. The population is ageing as older people live longer. An increasing proportion of homeless people have support needs that extend beyond the provision of housing. This is a major challenge for housing associations but one that must be approached with careful planning.

Housing support or care?

There is no clear definition of the boundaries of housing support, social care and personal care. It may include anything from more intensive housing management through to 24-hour nursing care. The housing can be anything from ordinary self-contained flats through to nursing homes. Some associations provide floating support or domiciliary care to tenants of other landlords or people who live in their own homes.

Over time associations have become involved in far more direct care and also much higher levels of care. This response to community needs has broadened relationships with local authorities. But it has been accompanied by increased operational complexity and risks. The housing culture and the care culture are significantly different. The particular staffing requirements, the complexity of the funding and contracting, and the different risks involved makes care and support a very different area of business from building and managing general needs housing. Housing associations in this field need executives and board members with the necessary skills and experience.

Partnerships

Housing associations have a long tradition of working in partnership to provide supported housing. While some associations provide specialist support or care themselves, others prefer just to provide accommodation and enter into agreements with partner agencies with specialist expertise in particular fields to provide support or care for residents.

Agreements with these partners can include management agreements, care contracts or leases. In some cases there are arrangements under which staff are seconded from one organisation to another. Getting partnership arrangements on to a secure and viable footing is one of the particular challenges of housing and care.

Employing care staff

Over 20,000 housing association staff are employed in the provision of care and support services and a substantial majority work in care homes. Many such staff work on shifts providing 24-hour care. The employment terms and conditions are necessarily different and involve features that would be beyond the experience of many associations. Training and support needs are also different and there is a need for flexibility as needs and contracts change. There is often the need for a wide range of scheme-based staff, such as nurses, general care staff, cooks and cleaners. Some residents can show violent or disturbing behaviour and this places particular demands on staff. High levels of expertise are required at a management level because of the requirement to know the needs of the client groups, as well as the complex funding and legislative framework.

Funding

Revenue funding is complex. Local authorities (at county or unitary level) fund housing-related support through Supporting People programmes. Higher levels of care are usually funded by social services departments and primary care trusts through care contracts. Increasingly contracts are competitively tendered.

Complex care arrangements may require a combination of special housing with the deployment of specialist staff. Because of the high costs of providing care, the funding arrangements are frequently revised. The revenue support is often on a one- to three-year basis and can be vulnerable to budget cuts. The removal of the ring fence from local authority care budgets in 2011 has intensified this vulnerability, adding to the general level of uncertainty and unpredictability.

For certain types of care, the funding goes with the client rather than the scheme. Social services departments enter into what are known as 'spot contracts' for the provision of a specified level of care for the individual. And as the government's personalisation initiative is rolled out, more and more individuals will receive personal budgets and personal payments with which to purchase their own care and support. Individual-based funding adds to the risks of organising the provision of care as there may be insufficient demand to cover the cost of the care capacity that the housing association has established.

Finding out more

The website of the Care Quality Commission is a good starting point for further information: www.cqc.org.uk.

For detailed information on the supply and performance of housing-related support services, visit the Communities and Local Government website: www.communities.gov.uk.

Chapter G

Working with tenants

Tenants are the principal consumers of a housing association's services. The term 'customer' is not always appreciated as tenants cannot easily take their custom away and shop elsewhere. Tenants often have very limited choices and there is a long history of landlords ignoring their views and preferences. It is this semi-monopoly position that gives an additional edge to the importance of involving tenants. It is vital that associations have effective ways of consulting and involving their tenants, and being accountable for the effectiveness of their services.

The experience of successfully convincing local authority tenants to transfer to housing associations or arms' length management organisations has had a profound effect on approaches to managing social housing and views about tenant involvement. This has occurred against a backdrop of the drive across the public sector to develop customer-oriented services that are tailored to the needs and preferences of citizens.

Some housing associations still find tenant involvement a challenge. Difficulties include keeping involvement going after activists move on, and a reluctance on the part of many tenants to get involved in formal participation structures. This is particularly true of groups such as young people, older people and black and ethnic minority tenants, whose voices have traditionally been less well heard by associations.

Why does effective involvement remain a challenge? Perhaps too much emphasis is placed on structures and methods, and too little on outcomes and the issues that really matter to tenants. Tenant involvement can become an end in itself rather than a means to improving services and performance.

There is increasing appreciation of the business case for using tenants' views, along with profile information and insight about tenants, to shape services. And increasing recognition that while obtaining tenants' views is important, it is crucial that mechanisms are in place to ensure that associations act on tenants' views and use them as a catalyst for driving forward improvement throughout the organisation.

G1 How does the partnership with tenants work?

In brief

A partnership approach involves offering tenants genuine opportunities to influence strategic priorities, housing-related policies and services and to scrutinise performance. Providers set out to agree with tenants how they will get involved and then provide support to help tenants build their capacity to be more effectively involved.

A partnership approach fundamentally alters the power relationship between landlords and tenants. It introduces an environment where tenants are genuinely listened to and have the power to effect change and make a real difference.

In more detail

Co-regulation

Traditionally tenants did not have much say in what services were provided or how they were provided. Professionals and politicians would decide on their behalf. Professor Martin Cave's 2007 review of housing association regulation proposed a new approach that places tenants at the heart of decisions about their homes and how services are delivered by their landlords. The Tenant Services Authority responded by introducing 'co-regulation' or self-regulation by providers involving and working with their tenants, subject to intervention by the regulator on a 'by exception' basis.

Co-regulation involves landlords and tenants working together locally to improve services, within a framework of National Standards set by the regulator. Key aspects of the approach are:

- housing association boards are responsible for effective service delivery;

- housing associations are accountable to tenants, not the regulator, for service delivery;

- clear outcome-focused National Standards;

- tenant involvement and transparency replace top-down guidance and instruction (all codes of practice, circulars and good practice guidance have been withdrawn);

- local offers (services and standards) that reflect local needs and priorities;

- transparent performance information so all stakeholders can easily see what is going on;

- self-assessment by landlords and scrutiny by tenants, backed up by external validation;

- a commitment to continuous improvement; and

- justified and proportionate intervention by the regulator, if required.

The Tenant Services Authority's regulatory framework marks a radical change in approach. Instead of waiting for, and then implementing, top-down guidance and instruction from the government or the regulator, landlords are now expected to work collaboratively with tenants and provide flexible and responsive services that are sensitive to the full range of tenants' needs. Some housing associations may need to time to adjust and get to grips with what this means in practice.

Improving the business

The partnership with tenants makes good business sense because it helps landlords to:

- understand and focus on what matters to tenants;

- shape services to match the full range of tenants' needs;

- get better value for money by concentrating on what tenants want and value;

- build better relationships between staff and tenants, and greater customer loyalty;

- deliver accountability to a customer group with little consumer choice;

- increase tenant satisfaction and meet targets with reduced risk.

Localism

Both the current and the previous government, in different ways, wish to encourage local control over and delivery of services. The Coalition Government's Big Society initiative seeks to empower individuals and communities to engage in society and shape change and improvement in their area. It is based on three pillars:

- social action (people giving time and money to help make life better);

- public service reform (involving charities, social enterprises and private companies in public service delivery); and

- community empowerment (devolving power to neighbourhoods).

It is seen as an alternative to the government trying to micro-manage everything from the centre. How it will work in practice is still evolving. However, the underlying principles are likely to guide the future direction of the government's social policy.

The Big Society dovetails neatly with co-regulation. As major providers of local publicly-funded services, housing associations and their tenants have the potential to make a major contribution, particularly in enabling people who are isolated or vulnerable to participate fully.

In terms of local communities, tenant involvement can have a powerful role to play in strengthening community cohesion, wellbeing and regeneration. Service provider initiatives (eg, social enterprises, regeneration plans) and consultation exercises can also offer tenants important personal development opportunities.

Finding out more

Excellence in service delivery and accountability: Code for members. National Housing Federation, 2010.

Making voices count: Reviewing practice in tenant involvement and empowerment. Tenant Services Authority, 2010.

The regulatory framework for social housing in England from April 2010. Tenant Services Authority, 2010.

G2   How can tenants be involved?

In brief

It is important to have effective ways of hearing from as many tenants as possible. This means offering a variety of different ways to be consulted and get involved that match tenants' different appetites and the amounts of time they are able to give. Typically, these range from occasional opportunities to give feedback through to actively taking part in managing services.

In more detail

At a time when organisations are under pressure to reduce costs while improving services, finding out what is important to tenants becomes crucial. Most housing associations go well beyond the legal minimum of consulting tenants on housing management matters, and seek tenants' views on many aspects of the services they provide and how tenants would like to see them improved. The different involvement methods include:

- feedback and expressing views (questionnaires, complaints, aspirations, telephone surveys, web surveys, focus groups, estate meetings etc.);

- ongoing discussion (tenants' and residents' associations, tenant panels etc.);

- service improvement activities (estate walkabouts, inspections, mystery shopping, scrutiny panels etc.);

- governance and direction setting (policy forums, service committees, boards etc.);

- community development activities (playgroups, youth activities, crime initiatives, regeneration partnerships etc.); and

- managing services (tenant management organisations).

Many of the different strands are complementary: formal structures provide an opportunity for collective discussion about issues, and customer research provides the quantitative evidence to help inform the discussion.

It is no criticism of tenants' associations and other tenant mechanisms to note that they often rely on the voluntary input of a relatively small number of tenants. The Tenant Involvement Commission found that most tenants want opportunities that are convenient and give a personal as well as a collective say. Only a minority are keen to be actively involved. Many more want to be involved when there is a key decision to be taken that is likely to affect them directly.

It is increasingly common for tenants to take a wider interest in the running of the organisation. This can be through involvement on area committees or functional committees and boards. Tenants on the board provide valuable insights into the organisation's services but should not be a substitute for more systematic involvement.

Finding out more

What Tenants Want: Report of the Tenant Involvement Commission, 2006. Available as a free download from www.housing.org.uk.

Housing: Improving services through resident involvement (report and management handbook). Audit Commission, 2004. Available as a download from www.audit-commission.gov.uk.

G3 What support might involved tenants expect?

In brief

Encouragement and support can help ensure that involved tenants are able to participate fully and make a worthwhile contribution that is of real value to the housing association and worth the time and effort involved. Help should be tailored to the type and level of involvement, and will usually require a combination of information, briefings, training, resources and ongoing guidance and support. Practical support will help sustain meetings or other activities, from refreshments, to help with travel or reimbursement for out-of-pocket expenses.

In more detail

Housing associations benefit by having as wide a range of tenants involved as possible. Achieving this requires a range of involvement methods that require different levels of commitment. Most tenants are only too happy to give their views about services, provided they feel it is worth the effort. Involvement which goes beyond giving occasional feedback or attending an occasional meeting is likely to require a combination of encouragement and support designed to enable:

- the broadest range of tenants as possible to get involved (internet as well as meetings, convenient locations, refreshments, out of pocket expenses etc.); and

- tenants to participate as fully and helpfully as possible.

Support needs to be tailored to the kind of involvement (one-off or ongoing, a consultative panel or a decision-making committee, mystery shopping, a scrutiny panel, a tenants' association etc.). It is likely to involve a mix of one or more of the following:

- convenient communication methods (face-to-face discussion, phone, internet etc.);

- a clear statement of the input required (role, likely time commitment etc.);

- information and briefings to bring tenants up to speed about what the task involves;

- training to enhance capacity and skills (committee skills, scrutiny, chairing etc.);

- careful planning of meetings to ensure time spent together is used to good effect (location, time of day, refreshments, agenda, background input, getting there etc.);

- guidance and hand holding (code of conduct, model tenants' association constitution, advice on dealing with difficult issues etc.);

- a simple way of claiming expenses to ensure that tenants are not out of pocket (travel, child care etc.); and

- access to resources (computers, internet, somewhere to keep papers etc.).

Being a representative, especially if someone is not experienced in acting on behalf of others, can be a daunting prospect. A coach or mentor can help tenants recognise the different roles that they play in different situations (board or scrutiny panel member or tenant activist) and how to perform them responsibly and work through any perceived conflicts of interest.

Perhaps the biggest encouragement is for tenants to feel that getting involved is worthwhile and does genuinely make a difference. Listening to what tenants have to say, and appreciating the time and effort involved, are important ingredients too.

Finding out more

Speak with either the company secretary or the resident involvement team about the range of support available to you and how you can access it.

Excellence in service delivery and accountability: Code for members. National Housing Federation, 2010 (see section I on 'empowerment and control' and section J on 'support for residents).

G4 How should the board relate to tenants and their organisations?

In brief

Boards must not expect tenant board members to be the channel for tenant views. Tenant board members do not represent tenants. Nor do they generally have constituencies to consult. The whole board needs to have mechanisms for relating to the whole tenant group. This will often involve regular joint meetings with tenant representatives or with a tenant forum or tenant panel, but also seeking out informal opportunities to meet with tenants.

In more detail

It is good practice for housing associations to encourage the establishment of tenants' associations by providing a model constitution and resources to meet routine running costs. Tenants' associations provide a basis for regular dialogue and enable tenants to be more proactive about the issues that concern them, rather than passive respondents to the organisation's consultation exercises. Larger housing associations will encourage groupings of tenants' associations into a federation or forum so that there is a body representing all of the organisation's tenants.

More recently, many organisations, together with their tenants, have also established scrutiny panels – these are stable groups of tenants working together to evaluate service performance and hold the organisation to account. Where these have been established, it is increasingly commonplace for the board to have an annual joint strategic planning session with the scrutiny panel, and for the chairs to meet regularly.

The board may also meet informally with tenants. Examples include board members attending annual tenant conferences; meeting with local groups of tenants on estate walkabouts; holding board meetings in local community centres with time built in before the meeting starts to liaise with local tenants.

A board may wish to consider more widely how its governance faces outwards, in particular how board decisions are communicated to tenants, and how tenants inform board thinking.

G5 What does 'scrutiny' mean?
In brief

'Scrutiny' means close inspection. It is the process of holding an organisation to account for performance. Tenant-led scrutiny gives tenants a formal role in self-regulation, together with the power to challenge the organisation and effect change. In practice, scrutiny means working collaboratively with other tenants and the executive to continuously improve performance. It is not the same as managing services, which is the executive's job.

In more detail

Scrutiny can involve a whole range of service improvement activities, such as inspections, mystery shopping, estate walkabouts or mystery shopping. Scrutiny panels generally add a layer of direction and co-ordination to these activities, along with a means of requiring the executive to take appropriate management action.

Scrutiny panels are usually designed to strengthen links between resident involvement activity and governance structures, to ensure that residents are able to influence decision-making processes. The purpose is to ensure that service delivery, at both operational and strategic levels, reflects the needs and aspirations of customers. However, it is important not to duplicate, cut across or undermine other performance review activities. The areas scrutinised must meet the needs of both tenants and the organisation, and so a mix of staff-selected and tenant-selected areas for scrutiny may be appropriate. The activities of the group may go beyond scrutiny, and include a role of ensuring that the resident voice is heard across the organisation.

Scrutiny can be seen as a symptom of doubt, and it is important to avoid undermining staff or putting them on the defensive. Everyone is on the same side and wants the best for the organisation. A collaborative approach generally works better than confrontation.

Scrutiny panels do not have the ability to exercise sanctions. They do not manage staff and cannot tell them what to do, or discipline them. The panel's task is to highlight inadequate performance, which then has to be picked up and acted upon by senior staff. While there might be capability issues, resolution is much more likely to require support or training, process or system changes, or additional resources or priority changes.

Finding out more

Resident-led self-regulation: Enhancing in-house scrutiny and performance by Abigail Davies and Mark Lupton. Chartered Institute of Housing, 2010 www.cih.org.

Making voices count: Reviewing practice in tenant involvement and empowerment. Tenant Services Authority, 2010.

Leading the way: Achieving resident-driven accountability and excellence, Richard Warrington and Davies, Abigail. Chartered Institute of Housing, 2007.

Chapter H

Property matters

Scale of activity

Over the last five years, housing associations have provided some 100,000 new rented homes. Shared ownership is now an increasingly significant part of most development programmes, along with key worker housing, intermediate market rent and even outright sale.

Type of activity

While development generally means building new homes or rehabilitating old ones, it does also cover remodelling existing homes and, where necessary, demolition.

Housing associations are increasingly involved in estate and neighbourhood regeneration, especially transfer associations. These can be very big projects which require close partnership with the local authority. In areas where housing associations are significant landlords, it is recognised that they have a 'place-shaping' role, ie, a responsibility to use their powers and influence to promote the well-being of local communities. Increasing concern for the environment and climate change has resulted in the *Code for Sustainable Homes*, alongside greater attention to cost in use and affordable warmth to mitigate the effects of rising energy prices.

As pressure has mounted to increase efficiency and achieve more with less, asset management has come to play an increasingly important role.

Funding

Over the last 20 years, the proportion of the cost of schemes met by grant has fallen from around 80 per cent to well below 50 per cent and is due to fall much further. The impact has been greatest on new build schemes. Lower levels of capital grant have led to higher rents.

These higher rents lead to higher levels of housing benefit. In effect, the lower the capital subsidy, the higher the level of revenue subsidy the government has to provide through housing benefit. This has had a number of undesirable side-effects. The most serious is that tenants are often caught in a poverty trap because income from low-paid employment reduces the level of housing benefit to which they are entitled. Proposals to increase rents to closer to market levels will exacerbate this problem.

Housing associations have become adept at finding ways to subsidise the cost of new homes and keep rents affordable, although the credit crunch exposed the consequences of relying on cross-subsidy from developers.

Restrictions on government funding mean that the availability of social housing grant for new homes is going to fall dramatically and disappear completely in many areas. This will usher in a new era that increases still further the pressure to deliver more with less; and where risks are higher, particularly in areas where social rents are already close to market levels. While the increased freedom and control over resources will be welcome, ensuring that rents continue to remain affordable by low income households will present an immense challenge to all housing associations.

H1   How are new homes developed?

In brief

Developing new homes requires four key ingredients:

- a development opportunity (site or building) that meets local authority priorities;

- the finance (grant, loan or reserves) to pay for the land and construction costs;

- tenants or owners to rent or buy the completed homes; and

- an acceptable level of risk.

In more detail

The purpose of development is to provide new homes for the people the housing association caters for. In most instances, this involves working in partnership with the local authority to meet local priorities, with the Homes and Communities Agency and other funders to secure the necessary resources, and increasingly with developers to secure some form of cross-subsidy.

As access to grant funding has become more and more difficult, development schemes have become increasingly complicated and difficult to deliver. In an effort to secure more social housing with less grant, registered providers are expected to explore all possible ways of minimising development costs, eg, land at less than market value, cross-subsidy, section 106 agreements (typically an obligation placed upon a developer to develop social housing as part of a wider development deal with the local authority).

Development is capital-intensive, takes a long time and rarely goes according to plan. There is a high risk of things going wrong, costing a lot more than originally budgeted, and taking a lot longer than originally planned. It is very important to have a method for undertaking and procuring the scheme that keeps risks within acceptable limits, also ensures that the homes are of an appropriate standard and, as far as it is possible to do so, that there will be tenants or owners willing to rent or buy the homes when they are completed.

Finding out more

Developing affordable housing: a guide to development and regeneration (2nd edition), Richard Broomfield and Drury, Andrew. National Housing Federation, 2009.

H2 How does the grant and finance framework work?
In brief

Housing associations that are registered providers are able to receive capital grants which enable them to charge below market rents. The balance of the capital cost has to be borrowed. The rent level has to cover the loan charges, housing management and maintenance costs and provision for future major repairs. Grants are also available for various forms of low cost home ownership.

The grant framework is changing. Rents are due to increase to closer to market levels and the level of subsidy is due to decrease dramatically. Increasingly, resources for developing new homes will come from surpluses made on housing associations' other stock.

In more detail

The Homes and Communities Agency and its role

The HCA is the government-sponsored public body that provides funding for housing and regeneration. The HCA works closely with local authorities to agree priorities and plans in each area. These take account of the local authority's strategic overview, needs assessment and place shaping. Housing associations are only one strand. The HCA sets design and quality standards that include meeting codes like the *Code for Sustainable Homes* and *Building for Life*. Providers have to qualify as a delivery partner to bid for funds.

Bidding for grant

The main social housing grant is called Social Housing Assistance (previous versions were called Social Housing Grant and Housing Association Grant). Other forms of grant assistance are available to contribute towards shared ownership, low cost home ownership, key worker housing, temporary housing and major repairs to pre-1988 funded stock.

In recent years the number of housing associations with development programmes has been declining. This is partly a consequence of competition for housing subsidy within an increasingly tough financial framework. Profit-making companies are also now eligible to become registered providers and to bid for capital grants. The intention of investment partnering is to reduce procurement costs and 'stretch' grant by:

● encouraging supply chain management through partnering between associations, suppliers and contractors;

- increasing the length of programmes to two, or possibly three, years so that there is a greater ability to plan ahead;

- encouraging the use of modern methods of construction (including timber frame, steel frame and prefabricated techniques); and

- encouraging partner associations to cross-subsidise the development of new homes.

Successful bidding is likely to depend on achieving the outputs required under local strategies for the least amount of grant subsidy.

Finding out more

The Homes and Communities Agency's *Affordable Housing Capital Funding Guide* is available online at http://cfg.homesandcommunities.co.uk.

H3   How does the development process work?
In brief

Development can seem a long-drawn-out process. Apart from securing a capital grant allocation, the proposed development must meet the HCA's design and quality standards and the housing association's own design and financial criteria. Schemes also have to be assessed against risk appraisal criteria before final commitments are made. The steps for each development include:

- identifying opportunities and buying land;

- deciding the brief (who it is for) and developing proposals for what is to be built on the site;

- financial and risk appraisal;

- obtaining planning permission;

- selecting the building contractor;

- supervising the construction;

- completion, handover and letting or sale;

- review.

In more detail

Buying land

Identifying sites which are likely to meet local authority, HCA and the housing association's own priorities will continue throughout the year.

The planning process

Planning approval is never a foregone conclusion. In all development work, uncertainty adds to the level of risk and delays can result in increased interest costs and the deferral of planned income. Supported housing schemes, in particular, can encounter planning difficulties as a result of objections from neighbours.

Going out to tender

Considerable work has been put into reducing the cost of development procurement and build costs. Partnering seeks to obtain cost savings by closer co-operation from the outset of a scheme. Securing competitiveness and quality in this situation is different from the traditional tendering route, and requires a high level of development expertise. Processes for selecting development partners (as with other large contracts) will need to comply with EU procurement rules.

In order to reduce risk, the organisation may enter into a design and build contract to reduce possible extra costs. The contractor will usually be selected through a process of competitive tendering which can take differing forms. Once the contract is awarded, the developing landlord will have commitments to meet payments, usually at certain stages defined in the contract. New build contracts will often last over 12 months. The contractor can usually complete the contract early, but will normally suffer penalties for late completion.

Rehabilitation generally involves contracts of a much lower value. However, there are higher levels of risk involved, as it is usually difficult to specify all the works that will be needed until the property has been acquired and any tenants have been re-housed.

The contract on site

Once the contractor has started work on the project, it is known as being 'on site'. Major building contracts can last 12 months or more.

Package deals

Package deals are where an organisation buys completed units. The contractor or architect takes all the risk, but the housing association has little or no say in standards and finishes. Often homes built for sale are less robust in construction and not designed to minimise cost in use.

> ## Finding out more
>
> *Developing affordable housing: A guide to development and regeneration (2nd edition)*, Richard Broomfield and Drury, A. National Housing Federation, 2009.

H4   What is the role of the board in development?

In brief

Development poses particular risks and requires close scrutiny. In small organisations, the board will be closely involved in every new development. In large organisations, the board's role is to set the framework and oversee implementation. Decisions can be delegated to a development committee or regional committees as well as to staff.

In more detail

The development committee

Developing housing associations often have a development committee to oversee development on behalf of the board. Typically development committees will be responsible for:

* development and procurement strategy;

* the policy and delivery framework (design standards, scheme appraisal criteria, approach to procurement and tendering, consultant and contractor panels, level of delegation to staff, contaminated land policy etc.);

* key partnerships or schemes that pose particular risks (schemes above delegated authority, schemes with no grant funding etc.);

* monitoring implementation of the programme (allocation take-up, cash spend, scheme costs, tenant feedback, contractor and consultant performance etc.).

One of the biggest challenges is to get the delegation right.

Links with finance and risk

Building development is a long-term, risky, capital-intensive activity. Long-term financial appraisal, risk appraisal and treasury management are crucial in ensuring that the organisation:

* has the necessary finance available (as reserves or borrowing) to pay for the development;

* will be able to afford to pay back any loans;

* will be able to pay for ongoing repairs and maintenance throughout the life of the building;

* will be able to cope with unforeseen outcomes or unexpected changes in interest rates.

H5   Can we develop without grant?
In brief

The development of housing without capital grant is possible but usually carries greater risks. There is generally some other form of subsidy involved like free or subsidised land, improvement grants, tax advantages, revenue grants, regeneration funds, or cross-subsidy from market-rented housing or reserves. There may be specialist niches where one or more of these subsidies can be combined with higher than usual rent levels and below average development costs. Property sales may also release funds to build new homes.

In more detail
Market and sub-market renting

Development without grant can be a matter of concern for private lenders, as the value of the tenanted scheme may not give them sufficient security for their loan. Higher rent levels in some parts of the country approach or even exceed market rents.

Student housing

Student housing and key worker housing are examples of schemes that have been successfully developed without capital grant. Sometimes associations with sufficient cash resources will choose to invest them in schemes without the benefit of grant, even though they might secure a better rate of return by putting the money on deposit with a financial institution. More usually, housing associations with surplus resources will choose to gear up their investment by using it as a means for securing grant that might not otherwise be available.

H6   How do PFI, regeneration, and stock transfer work?
In brief

The Private Finance Initiative (PFI) and stock transfer are different vehicles for borrowing of the capital finance necessary to undertake major regeneration or new build schemes.

In more detail
Stock transfer

Stock transfer involves the transfer of the ownership of a local authority's housing stock to a housing association alongside raising the capital finance required to refurbish the stock so that homes meet the Decent Homes Standard.

Transfers of the whole stock are called large scale voluntary transfers. Partial transfers of, for example, an estate might be to a Local Housing Company. Usually the transfer is to a new housing association especially created to accept the transfer. Sometimes the new association is a subsidiary of an existing housing association.

LSVTs are a particular form of housing association. The boards are made up of one-third tenants, one-third local authority representatives and one-third independent members. Transfers involve detailed 30-year business plans outlining the level of funding required and demonstrating how the new organisation will repay the loans. A majority of tenants have to vote in favour for a transfer to proceed. Transfers usually contain guarantees limiting rent increases for the first few years.

Private Finance Initiative

The Private Finance Initiative uses private finance as part of a public-private partnership. A public sector organisation contracts with a private sector entity (usually a consortium) to purchase services, at a defined scale and standard, on a long-term basis. The consortium constructs the necessary facilities and provides the associated services for the life of the contract. The number of PFI projects increased rapidly after 1997.

The HCA is responsible for delivering the housing PFI programme. In housing PFI, local authorities contract with private sector firms to build or improve, and then manage and maintain, social housing. Contracts are typically for 25-30 years. While management of the housing stock becomes the responsibility of the private sector contractor, the local authority continues to own the housing and retains the tenants. PFI has also been used to provide new care homes.

The aim of PFI is to harness private sector management and expertise in the delivery of public services, while reducing the impact on public borrowing of providing these services, and transferring risk to the private sector. There have been doubts as to whether PFI projects genuinely represent value for money and whether risks genuinely transfer to the private sector. The credit crunch has had a serious impact on the supply of finance for new projects.

Finding out more

Further information about stock transfer and housing PFI is available from the Homes and Communities Agency at: www.homesandcommunities.co.uk.

H7 What is 'asset management'?

In brief

'Asset management' involves taking a comprehensive approach to managing a housing association's physical assets with the aim of achieving particular objectives, usually to make best use of the housing stock and achieve value for money. It covers the construction, operation, maintenance, modification, replacement and disposal of housing and other buildings. It can also include other assets like physical infrastructure, IT systems, and so on.

In more detail

A comprehensive approach

Asset management involves taking a comprehensive approach to achieving value for money across both revenue expenditure (response repairs, cyclical repairs, voids, adaptations etc.) and capital expenditure (investment in improvement and replacement of roofs, windows, heating systems, kitchens and bathrooms etc.) over the life of the building. This is likely to involve adopting a programmed approach to repairs. It may also involve the disposal of buildings that are expensive to manage or maintain, or are in poor condition and not financially worthwhile to repair, or have a very high value on the open market that is disproportionate to their social housing value, or do not make a sufficient contribution to achieving the housing association's overall objectives.

Stock swaps and rationalisation

Widely dispersed stock is difficult to manage and maintain effectively. It also costs more per home than if stock is concentrated in an area. Landlords with a small presence in a locality also find it difficult to play a full part in the community. They do not have the resources to develop effective partnerships with the local authority and other local landlords to deal with neighbourhood issues, community liaison, partnership working etc. They also have limited capacity to work with their tenants and respond effectively to local priorities.

Increasingly housing associations are forming views about their future role in an area. And if they conclude that they do not have a sufficient presence in an area, some are deciding to withdraw and explore options to rationalise their stock holdings. Sometimes this can be achieved by swapping properties with another housing association, or alternatively through the sale of the properties to a local housing association.

Chapter J

The board as an employer

For all organisations that employ staff, effective service delivery depends primarily on the quality and effectiveness of the staff involved. Effective human resource management is essential to success. The diversity of housing associations means that a few now employ thousands of staff, while the majority employ fewer than five staff. Along with these differences in size go differences in structure and salary levels.

The organisation's general approach to human resource management will be governed by its mission and organisational values. In larger organisations, this will involve setting the framework and monitoring implementation. In smaller organisations, board members are likely to have a more active role in implementation. Key aspects of undertaking the role of employer are:

- human resource management (strategy and policy for all matters relating to the recruitment, reward, retention, motivation and development of the housing association's staff);

- talent management (staff training, personal development, performance management, management development, succession, HR aspects of organisational learning and knowledge etc.);

- employee relations (contracts of employment, staff handbooks, HR policies, disciplinary and grievance procedures, union recognition etc.);

- monitoring and scrutiny (training, sickness, turnover, reasons for leaving etc.);

- equality and diversity; and

- health and safety.

J1   What are the board's legal responsibilities as an employer?

In brief

As the ultimate employer, the board is responsible for ensuring that the housing association complies with employment law. A key principle is to act fairly and reasonably.

Employment law is complex and constantly evolving. Board members need to understand and keep up to date with their legal responsibilities as an employer and the implications for the housing association. The chief executive and other senior managers should, as part of their role, keep the board informed about changes in legal requirements and make sure that policies, procedures and other arrangements comply with them.

In more detail

Employment law

As a general rule employment law applies to all organisations regardless of the number of employees. European law is having an increasing impact. Sometimes it is not clear how regulations will work in practice until a tribunal has ruled on interpretation.

Statutory provisions cover maternity, paternity and adoption leave and absence, equal opportunities, working hours and overtime, flexible working, health and safety, pay, sick pay, harassment and bullying, conduct and disciplinary action. Employers also have a general duty of care towards employees to provide a safe place to work. Employees have a duty to comply with reasonable instructions and with the organisation's policies and procedures. It is wise to ensure that terms and conditions are communicated to employees to reduce the scope for misinterpretation later. Discrimination and fair and unfair dismissal are particularly sensitive risks.

Organisations will want to be clear about who is an employee and who is a contractor, and will generally want to ensure that outsourcing partners meet the housing association's policies.

The contract of employment

All staff are entitled to a written statement of the terms and conditions of their employment as a matter of law. These include name, date employment commenced, job title, remuneration, hours of work, holiday entitlement and place of work. There are further requirements that are usually included in a staff handbook. These include sickness provisions, pensions, notice, end date if fixed term, collective agreements, and dismissal, disciplinary and grievance procedures.

The minimum requirements are primarily to protect employees. Prudent employers will have additional provisions in their written contracts and staff handbooks that reflect the needs of their business. These might include benefits and expenses, drugs and alcohol, use of facilities like the telephone and email, training, right of search, confidentiality and data protection, taking on external work, and whistle blowing.

TUPE

The Transfer of Undertakings (Protection of Employment) Regulations 2006 (TUPE) apply to two broad types of transfer: business transfers and changes in service provision. The regulations are designed to protect employees in transfer situations and ensure that they continue to enjoy the same terms and conditions and continuity of employment. TUPE is a complex area so it is essential to identify the key risks and seek legal advice at the earliest possible stage. Organisations cannot prevent TUPE applying, but it is common practice for old and new employers to agree how to divide the liabilities that arise.

Finding out more

Employment rights on the transfer of an undertaking: A guide to the 2006 TUPE Regulations for employees, employers and representatives. Department for Business Innovation and Skills, 2009: www.bis.gov.uk.

J2   What are the key aspects to consider?

In brief

The organisation's overall approach will include the staffing structure, getting the right people, ensuring salaries and benefits remain competitive, appraisal and training and development.

In more detail

Staff structure

There is no ideal staff structure. The structure needs to suit the housing association's particular role and resources and adapt to changing circumstances. At the least, it should provide clarity of roles and responsibilities so that all staff and board members know who is responsible for what. When reviewing the structure, board members will need to consider:

- the balance between span of control (too wide and the staff being managed will lack support and supervision) and the number of management tiers (too many and control becomes extended and inflexible);

- reconciling functional efficiency (by working in functional departments such as housing services, development, finance etc.) and geography. Most smaller and medium-sized housing associations are organised on functional lines. Larger organisations have more decentralised operations. Housing associations working across wide areas often develop a regional or area structure within which there is more generic working.

It is almost certainly more important to build effective teams than to have the perfect structure. Repeated reorganisations are disruptive and demotivating.

For housing associations with few staff members, each new post will be a major step to be considered by the board. As the organisation grows, there will be key stages when it needs to establish a management team and a degree of middle management. Once there is a chief executive and management team, the board will set overall limits on the staff establishment and approve major reorganisations. It will tend not to get involved in more detailed staff structure issues.

Getting the right people

Housing associations seek the best staff that they can afford at all levels. While this necessarily involves salary issues, it is also about effective recruitment. Key elements include:

- Define the job, the required skills and competencies. A clear statement of the role and the qualities and experience needed to undertake it should be set out in a job description and person specification or in a role profile and competency framework that includes the required level of performance. The degree of detail will help ensure the organisation recruits the right person and is able to performance manage them if required

- Attract the best applicants. In most circumstances, jobs should be advertised openly (both internally and externally). The choice of advertising media will depend on the nature of the job

- A selection process that is fair and designed to assess the ability of candidates to undertake the job. Interviews alone are not sufficient, even when well structured, to cover all key areas. It is good practice to use a combination of exercises and tests

- Objectivity and fairness are essential and key to getting the best person. The requirements for the post must not be drawn up in such a way as to discriminate (except where this is specifically permitted by law). All stages of the recruitment process should be monitored and documented so that the organisation can check that it is not inadvertently discriminating and can respond to any concerns raised by candidates

- Comprehensive induction for all new staff.

Salaries and terms and conditions

Associations will want to be satisfied that they offer sufficiently competitive salaries and benefits to attract and retain competent staff at all levels without wasting scarce resources. This requires the organisation to have:

- salaries that are linked to the value of the job;

- a pay structure that is fair and appropriate (usually grades with a set number of salary points, and fixed salary points for senior staff);

- employee benefits that are typical for the sector;

- no inappropriate gap between the chief executive and other staff (senior management skills are expensive and have become more important as organisations have grown in size. It can be helpful for the board to get an independent perspective on senior management pay from time to time);

- recognition of performance (performance-related pay systems are not common, but performance is normally taken into account at a senior management level – either through a modest bonus system or in the annual pay review);

- market monitoring to ensure salaries and benefits remain competitive (many housing associations are members of benchmarking clubs and share data on employee benefits).

Pay is a sensitive issue for housing associations. It is the main determinant of an organisation's cost base and care must be taken not to waste resources. Boards need to take particular care of the payments that are made in the contexts of terminating executive employment contracts. The regulator expects housing associations to avoid excessive or inappropriate pay-offs. Associations must be aware of exactly how regulatory requirements will apply and whether there are relevant exemptions. This is an area in which boards should seek external advice.

Performance appraisal

It is good practice for housing associations to have appraisal systems. It is important that skills development and performance targets are consistent with the organisation's objectives. A clear policy will enable employees to see how appraisal links to training and development, and reward if relevant.

Training and development

Training is important for staff at all levels. The competence of the employee group is critical to the success of the organisation and the sector and in the management of risk. Properly skilled employees help minimise risks. Access to training and development can be a useful retention mechanism. Setting out a clear policy will help to manage employee expectations.

Finding out more

It is normal for a board or a delegated committee to receive information on overall performance in personnel – staff turnover, sickness, approach to appraisal etc. Review the last report or speak to the person with overall responsibility for organisational development to learn more about the organisation's approach to growing its staff.

You may also want to consider some training on the board's role as an employer.

J3   Working with the staff team

In brief

The key partnership for any housing association is the one between the board and staff. Achieving a productive and mutually supportive relationship that serves the needs of the organisation requires both clarity of roles and ongoing relationship building. While the relationship will vary with the size and complexity of the organisation's operations, the board's main role is to provide overall direction, and the senior staff are responsible for the day-to-day management.

In more detail

Forging a genuine partnership

Overall direction is particularly concerned with strategy, objectives and the delegation framework. Management is about achieving objectives through the day-to-day management of operations. Against this background, there is plenty of scope for misunderstandings and the development of a 'them and us' attitude.

While the board has overall responsibility for the organisation's affairs, this does not imply that an autocratic style of direction is appropriate. 'We tell them what to do and they do it' is not a recipe for a productive board/staff relationship. Housing associations (along with other organisations that have social objectives) can generate strong staff commitment to their work. This needs to be harnessed and sustained rather than undermined. Board members also have limited time. The staff have the access to information and the time to develop proposals, and should also have all the professional skills required.

Equally it is important to avoid a situation in which the board feels that it is just a rubber stamp and the staff feel that they are subject to the random rejection and amendment of sound proposals. Both roles have to be worthwhile if they are to work effectively and to their full potential. This requires both an understanding and respect for the respective roles and a willingness to share power. A partnership approach is best, where strategies, objectives and policies are developed jointly and, as far as possible, in a way that emphasises the shared commitment of both the board and staff.

The distinction between the board's role of directing and the chief executive's role of managing can only be taken so far. There is, inevitably, fertile ground for disputing where the boundary lies. Earned trust, mutual respect and a concern to ensure that both board members and senior staff have fulfilling roles are good starting points. It will also be of great benefit to establish agreed mechanisms for putting these sentiments into practice.

The balance of challenge and support

Organisations whose boards and staff are a mutually supportive partnership tend to be more innovative and better able to cope with problems and setbacks. Board meetings also achieve positive results. But where these core relationships are strained, a great deal of energy goes into sniping and back-covering. Problems and setbacks become a battlefield rather than matters to be resolved and overcome. Board meetings achieve little and staff and board members alike feel drained.

In terms of achieving aims and objectives, the board wants senior staff to understand clearly what the board requires, to focus on what is important and devise an effective plan for achieving it, to give the plan the priority and resources that will ensure it is delivered, to be open about any issues or difficulties and to report back on progress.

The purpose of challenge is to identify underlying issues and, where there are difficulties or performance issues, ensure that an effective plan is in place to remedy them. A supportive approach is to ask open questions and invite staff to explain. There might be capability issues, but it is much more likely that the difficulty can be resolved by support and training, process or system changes, additional resources or changes in priorities.

Managing boundaries

Respecting the management line means that instructions to staff should always be routed through their line manager. This applies to the board in relation to the chief executive as much as it does to other managers.

> ### Finding out more
>
> It is useful to include executive staff in annual board appraisals, so that both groups can review the board's effectiveness and the strength of their relationship. Find out if your approach to appraisal includes senior staff.

J4   What does 'organisational culture' mean?

In brief

'Organisational culture' is a term used to describe how an organisation behaves and organises itself: the values, norms, customs, traditions, rules and procedures that give an organisation its own particular feel and ways of working. Every organisation has its own unique culture.

In more detail

What culture means

'Organisational culture' encompasses the values and norms that are shared by people and groups in an organisation and that determine the way they interact with each other and with other people both inside and outside the organisation. It sets the standards of behaviour required. It is the feel we get when we walk into an organisation, whether it is fast moving and responsive, or whether it feels old and backward looking.

'Values' determine the kinds of goals to pursue and set appropriate standards of behaviour. 'Norms' (guidelines or expectations) specify appropriate kinds of behaviour for employees in particular situations and towards one another.

An example of the impact of different cultures can be seen in the different approaches that housing associations take to tenant involvement. A key issue, when considering approaches to tenant involvement, is whether an organisation sees tenant involvement as the domain of specific employees or a particular section of the organisation, or as being about embedding a culture of positive interaction with tenants throughout the whole organisation; that tenant involvement is a matter for all staff, not just certain specific employees who are tenant involvement officers.

The role of the board

The board takes a lead in setting organisational culture. Board members should seek to embody and reinforce the values of the organisation and convey a consistent tone and set an example.

Finding out more

Better than before: The improvement journey, Campbell Tickell. Tenant Services Authority, 2010: www.tenantservicesauthority.org.

Engaging for Success: enhancing performance through employee engagement. David MacLeod and Nita Clarke, Department for Business, Innovation and Skills, 2009.

J5 Why does health and safety matter so much?

In brief

Ensuring that employees are safe and healthy at work is a fundamental aspect of being a responsible employer. The legal requirements about health and safety are extensive, and organisations that fail to comply risk facing substantial penalties. Housing associations that invest in the health and well-being of their staff will also benefit from enhanced employee commitment, reduced levels of absence and greater staff retention.

In more detail

The legal responsibilities

The principal legislation is the Health and Safety at Work Act 1974. It requires employers to do everything reasonably practicable to provide a safe and healthy workplace and adequate welfare facilities. The act is supported by extensive regulations, guidance and codes of practice. Employers also have a common law duty of care to protect their employees, provide a safe working environment and recruit competent and safety conscious staff. Health and safety includes assessing and taking steps to minimise the risks associated with accidents, illness and disease, as well as managing work-life balance.

Penalties for non-compliance can include both heavy fines and imprisonment. Board members can be prosecuted for corporate manslaughter if gross failure to take reasonable care for the safety of staff or the public results in a person's death.

Putting health and safety at the core

Building sites are particularly dangerous, and offices can contain a surprising number of hazards if not properly supervised. All organisations should have an appropriate manager responsible for overall issues of health and safety and a designated health and safety officer for every office and location where staff are employed. A regular assessment of health and safety risks should be carried out and steps taken to implement its recommendations.

Finding out more

For further information, visit the website of the Health and Safety Executive, www.hse.gov.uk.

Ask to see your organisation's health and safety policy, and any relevant performance reports.

J6 How do we uphold equality and diversity?

In brief

Housing associations must comply with equality legislation and avoid discriminating against an employee or job applicant on any of the prohibited grounds. This requires implementing policies and taking action to eliminate discrimination and ensure that everyone is treated fairly and respectfully. A welcoming and inclusive approach also helps to attract the best talent.

It is important that associations practise what they preach in the way that they manage their work and employ staff. Equality of opportunity is also an issue for the composition of the board.

In more detail

The legal responsibilities

The Equality Act 2010 brings together and streamlines over 100 different Acts of Parliament, regulations, guidance and codes of practice that deal with protection from discrimination, harassment and victimisation. The Act offers protection to people affected by nine 'protected characteristics':

- age (includes both older and younger persons);

- disability (includes physical, sensory, mental health and learning disabilities);

- gender reassignment ('trans' or 'transgender');

- marriage and civil partnership;

- pregnancy and maternity;

- race;

- religion or belief;

- sex; and

- sexual orientation.

It is unlawful for an employer to discriminate against, harass or victimise an employee or a person seeking work on grounds of a protected characteristic. Except in very specific situations, an employer must not ask about a job applicant's health until the person has either been offered a job (on a conditional or unconditional basis) or included in a pool of successful candidates to be offered a job when a suitable position arises.

Organisations have a duty to make 'reasonable adjustments' to enable disabled people to take up or continue to work for an organisation or to gain access to the services an organisation provides. This may mean changing how things are done, or providing access to a building or providing auxiliary aids.

Service providers may treat disabled people more favourably than people who are not disabled. So a landlord may give priority to disabled people when carrying out repairs. Disability discrimination is discrimination due to the effect of a disability rather than on grounds of the disability itself.

The Act recognises that having a 'protected characteristic' may, in some limited circumstances, be a real asset for some jobs. The employee must be providing intensive one-to-one support to people with the same protected characteristic. For example, a hostel worker working with female victims of domestic abuse might have to be a female in order to avoid causing further distress to clients.

Monitoring

The purpose of monitoring is to identify issues that affect staff and measure change over time. Monitoring enables employers to examine the make-up of the workforce, highlight differences between groups across teams and grades, and identify and tackle discrimination.

Monitoring also helps normalise less familiar characteristics like sexuality and creates a more inclusive workplace by demonstrating to employees that the organisation values diversity.

Monitoring is concerned with performance. Customer insight, and knowing and understanding who the organisation's customers are and what they want, are important too.

Not just an 'extra'

There is growing awareness of the business case for having a diverse workforce and the central part that equality and diversity policies play in achieving this. The ability to deliver responsive, personalised services will depend in a large part on the composition, skills, understanding and commitment of the workforce. It is vital that staffing strategies and employment policies include relevant equality and diversity objectives, and training and development programmes address equality issues.

Finding out more

Equality Act 2010 Guidance for service providers: What equality law means for your voluntary and community sector organisation (including charities and religion or belief organisations), Equality and Human Rights Commission, 2010: www.equalityhumanrights.com.

J7 Is it worth going for employer awards?

In brief

Employer awards usually involve some form of audit and can be a useful way of developing a more systematic approach to organisational development. Awards can also help give associations a competitive edge when recruiting for skilled staff in a tight labour market.

In more detail

Some awards, through including an employee survey as part of their approach, help organisations to look at how things work from the employee's point of view.

Investors in People

Many associations have found it helpful to go through the process of obtaining Investors in People accreditation as a way of developing a more systematic approach to training and development, listening to staff, and then getting recognition for their achievement.

Two ticks: a symbol and the words 'positive about disabled people'

Some organisations apply for use of this symbol in order to understand how well they perform in recruitment, training, retention, consultation and disability awareness.

Industry awards

There are a number of annual award ceremonies in the sector organised by different interest groups and bodies. Even when the housing association is not a winner, the attention brought to staff teams or individuals can be an important morale booster.

The Sunday Times Best 100 Companies to work for (and similar such awards)

Some organisations like to measure their performance as an employer not only against housing peers, but against other private and public sector employers. A number of organisations who have been through this process several times report that the first assessment helps them to identify and work on areas of weaker performance.

Finding out more

www.investorsinpeople.co.uk.

www.bestcompanies.co.uk.

www.housing.org.uk.

J8 How should a board go about appointing a new chief executive?

In brief

For housing associations employing staff, there are few more important decisions that a board can take than the appointment of the organisation's chief executive. High calibre staff are essential to achieve objectives. A high calibre chief executive and senior management team are also a key protection for board members against the risks inherent in running a substantial operation. Best practice is to ensure a range of candidates through open recruitment, and to delegate the appointment to a small panel of experienced board members. It is vital that all candidates should be treated fairly, and that their confidentiality should be protected.

In more detail

The appointment process

Most boards will have infrequent experience of chief executive recruitment. Professional advice on how to attract the best candidates, what to pay them and how to test them thoroughly is widely accepted as good practice. The board should also delegate the appointment to a panel of its most experienced members. The recruitment process needs careful timetabling and design to ensure that it works as well as possible. The stages of the process could include some or all of:

- a first-stage filtering interview, at which a longlist of candidates is seen, to create a shortlist of (say) three to five candidates;

- psychometric tests and exercises;

- visits to properties and projects, with opportunities to meet tenants and staff;

- informal meetings with senior staff and the outgoing chief executive – note that it is not good practice for these to be involved in the final decision;

- an opportunity to meet with the wider board membership, for instance at a dinner or other event; and

- a formal interview, with a presentation to the selection panel.

Test and exercises

Many organisations find it helpful to test candidates, using psychometric tests to check on such things as:

- numerical and verbal reasoning;

- ability to prioritise; and/or

- leadership and personal style.

Such tests can now be conducted online, and provide useful information that can be probed at interview. Test results should be taken into account as a part of the overall process, but not give undue weight in the final decision.

Interviewing

It is good practice for all the interviews to be conducted in the same way, using an agreed list of questions. Some form of marking or scoring can be useful. Panel members who are not experienced interviewers should be given training in diversity, equality and interview techniques.

Internal candidates

Internal candidates should be treated fairly and equally with other candidates, neither advantaged nor disadvantaged.

Making the decision

The decision should be made on a fair and objective basis, using the results of the interviews, tests, and the information provided by candidates in their applications.

J9   How should a chief executive be appraised?
In brief

The best approach is for a small group of board members or a remuneration committee to oversee the chief executive's appraisal. This allows the chief executive's relationship with the chair to be one of the aspects reviewed. Appraisal works best if it includes:

- an element of self-appraisal;

- an opportunity to share concerns;

- taking account of the views of other colleagues and board members;

- an opportunity for both parties to discuss difficulties; and

- agreed conclusions and targets for the future.

The outcome should be shared with the board as a whole.

In more detail
Setting targets

To get the best value from an appraisal process, it needs to be structured. The measures of performance need to be agreed in advance, as well as the format of the process. The measures of performance for a chief executive are likely to include:

- key targets and objectives from the corporate and business plans;

- the effectiveness of the relationship with the board (which goes beyond efficient servicing);

- the effective management of the senior management team; and

- other main duties set out in the job description.

Giving feedback

All board members should be invited to give feedback about the chief executive's performance. The process will need to be co-ordinated. Often other executive members give feedback too.

The appraisal process provides a valuable opportunity for the chief executive to hear members' views about his or her performance, both good and where there is scope to improve. All members should do their best to contribute. Feedback works best if it is balanced and includes praise for what has been done well. Any criticism should be as specific as possible and include suggestions for ways to improve.

Finding out more

Make sure that you are clear about the process used in your organisation to assess the chief executive's performance and how board members contribute to that assessment. Ensure that you understand how objectives for the executive are set.

J10 how should we set the chief executive's pay package?
In brief

The board is responsible for determining the remuneration of the chief executive. If, as is increasingly common, the pay of the chief executive and senior managers takes account of performance, then it is particularly important for the appraisal of performance to be systematic and accountable.

In more detail
The annual process

Senior management remuneration is best delegated to a remuneration committee but it is normally for the board as a whole to approve the chief executive's remuneration package.

Getting external help

Associations should take advice so as to ensure that the chief executive's remuneration package (and that of other senior executives) is competitive but not excessive.

Bonuses and incentives

Remuneration is not just about salary. Terms and conditions of employment need to be reviewed periodically.

Finding out more

You may wish to look at the last external adviser's report benchmarking your chief executive's pay.

J11 Should the board be involved in other employment matters?

In brief

Generally the board's role is to support the chief executive in implementing the board's employment policies. In smaller housing associations with less experienced senior managers and only a few staff, the board has to get much more involved in managerial issues including employment matters. Sometimes board members or other volunteers carry out the day-to-day work.

In more detail

Supporting the chief executive

The board may have a functional committee, or a particular board member who takes the lead on employment matters. One or more members may have expert knowledge and be in a position to give expert advice. Sometimes board members have a role as part of collective bargaining arrangements, or in hearing employment appeals.

Other senior staff appointments

The board has a legitimate interest in the appointment of other members of the senior management team. However, it is the chief executive who manages the other members of the team. Board members on an interview panel should be very wary of imposing their choice on a reluctant chief executive.

The appraisal of other senior managers is the primary responsibility of the chief executive. However, the board will want to know that there is a robust appraisal system, that appraisals are taking place in a timely way and that its own concerns have been aired. Many associations are now using '360 degree' appraisal systems that seek views from those who are managed by the appraisee as well as those of the appraisee's manager.

J12 What happens if staff aren't performing?

In brief

Occasionally problems arise in the relationship between the board and senior staff or between the chair and chief executive. It should usually be possible for these to be dealt with informally between the chair and chief executive. Effective appraisal systems should help to address such problems before they become too serious. However, occasionally serious problems can arise and present a non-executive board with particular difficulties. External advice should always be sought if the board concludes that the problems are insurmountable.

In more detail
The special position of the chief executive
The board should recognise that all senior management problems involve the chief executive, and that the board itself may not be completely blameless. If the problems lie at second tier level then the board should support the chief executive in resolving them. A chief executive who does not tackle them effectively becomes the more serious part of the problem.

Where the problem arises with the chief executive then the burden of resolving it falls on the board. Problems can arise in many ways. For example, the demands of the job may have outgrown the individual or there may have been a breakdown in the key working relationship with the chair or other board members.

If, for any reason, the relationship is not working effectively the board should seek external advice before taking precipitate action. Difficulties may stem from a breakdown in the chair/chief executive relationship rather than performance in other aspects of the role. Seeking external advice at an early stage can help clarify the root causes of the difficulties and identify the best approach to successfully resolving them.

Disciplinary and capability procedures
Boards are always reluctant to use disciplinary or capability procedures. Their use is an acknowledgement that the problems are serious and may accentuate an existing poor relationship. However, a failure to follow formal procedures will put the board in the wrong if the matter is not resolved by agreement and results in dismissal. The board's position is made even harder if the disciplinary and capability procedures are inappropriate for senior managers. If matters reach this stage then the board is likely to find it helpful to seek external advice.

When people have to leave
The cost of continuing poor management can be substantial. It saps the morale of staff and board alike and diverts energy and attention away from other issues. It can lead to progressive deterioration of performance and expensive mistakes. The cost of inaction is likely to be far greater than the cost of an agreed parting of the ways or even of losing an employment tribunal action.

It is particularly important to seek external advice if compensation payments might become involved, as there may be regulatory or moral constraints on the level of severance payments.

Where to find out more

K1 National and local networks

Name	Description	Web address
Charity Commission for England and Wales	Body that registers and regulates charities.	www.charity-commission.gov.uk
Chartered Institute of Housing (CIH)	Professional body for housing staff.	www.cih.org
Confederation of Co-operative Housing (CCH)	Umbrella body for housing co-operatives.	www.cch.coop
Homes and Communities Agency	National housing and regeneration agency.	www.homesandcommunities.co.uk
Housing Ombudsman Service (HOS)	The statutory ombudsman service for housing associations.	www.housing-ombudsman.org.uk
National Council for Voluntary Organisations (NCVO)	Umbrella body for voluntary organisations in England. Website includes guidance for trustees on a wide range of practical and legal issues.	www.ncvo-vol.org.uk.
National Housing Federation	Trade body for housing associations	www.housing.org.uk
National Federation of ALMOs	Trade body for ALMOs.	www.almos.org.uk
National Federation of Tenant Management Organisations (NFTMOs)	Umbrella body for tenant management organisations.	www.nftmo.com

Name	Description	Web address
Tenant Participation Advisery Service (TPAS)	National membership organisation for tenants and landlords.	www.tpas.org.uk
Tenant Services Authority	The regulator of social housing (until April 2012).	www.tenantservicesauthority.org

K2 The trade press

The main housing journal is called *Inside Housing*, and appears weekly, on a Friday. Most housing associations will arrange for board members to receive a subscription to their home addresses.

There are also other journals and magazines, relating to housing, building regeneration, planning and regeneration.

K3 Training

The National Housing Federation provides a good range of training courses for board members and others, as does the Chartered Institute of Housing. Many organisations run their own in-house training programmes, sometimes in partnership with other local providers.

In addition, there is any number of commercial and voluntary organisations providing training services. These will often be advertised in *Inside Housing*.

K4 Conferences and events

The National Housing Federation runs an annual programme of conferences, including one for board members, usually in January or early February. The main annual conference is in September.

The Chartered Institute of Housing's main conference is in June, and there are also some well-attended regional events.

Index